The Great Depression

The Great Depression

Lionel Robbins

With a new introduction by Murray Weidenbaum

Transaction Publishers
New Brunswick (U.S.A.) and London (U.K.)

Library of Congress Catalog Number: 2009000212
ISBN: 978-1-4128-1008-1
Printed in the United States of America

Library of Congress Cataloging-in-Publication Data

Robbins, Lionel Robbins, Baron, 1898-1984
    The great depression / Lionel Robbins ; with a new introduction by Murray Weidenbaum.
        p. cm.
    Originally published: London : Macmillan and co., limited, 1934.
    ISBN 978-1-4128-1008-1
        1. Economic history--1918-1945 2. Currency question.
    3. Depressions--1929. 4. Currency question--Great Britain.
    5. United States--Economic policy. I. Title.

HC57.R57 2009
330.9'043--dc22

                                                    2009000212

TO

I. E. R.

CONTENTS

THE GREAT DEPRESSION

CONTENTS

CHAPTER VII

RESTRICTIONISM AND PLANNING

CHAPTER VIII

CONDITIONS OF RECOVERY

CHAPTER IX

PROSPECTS

TABLES IN THE
STATISTICAL APPENDIX

THE GREAT DEPRESSION

INTRODUCTION TO THE
TRANSACTION EDITION

LIONEL ROBBINS was one of the giants among British economists over the past century and a star at the London School of Economics. His classic work, *Essay on the Nature and Significance of Economic Science*, is still a staple on the reading lists assigned to graduate students of economics. In contrast, his later work, *The Great Depression*, has become a neglected period piece.

As the reader of this volume will quickly learn, however, there is much of value to those concerned with the contemporary challenges facing the American economy as well as the global marketplace. Before I draw attention to the more obvious lessons for today, it is fitting to pay tribute to the style as well as content of *The Great Depression*.

Unlike most recent studies of economic history and policy, Lord Robbins writes in clear English readily understood by educated readers not especially trained in formal economics. There is no shortage of statistical tables (36) and charts (7), but it does not require proficiency in econometrics to follow them. Robbins brightens this book with allusions to Shakespeare, the Bible, and an apt quotation from the poet Alexander Pope.

Reading Robbins somehow is reminiscent of the great actor Charles Laughton reciting from the New York telephone book. Laughton converted the most ordinary prose to high drama. In a comparable manner, Robbins describes economic developments in language that makes readers feel that they are reading classical literature. Rather than merely describing the fluctuations of the business cycle, he writes of the recurrent waves of business depression and unemployment, which "ruffle the lines of secular development." Indeed, allusions to the pyramids of the Pharaohs alternate with descriptions of the division of labor.

However, it is the continuing relevance of the substance of *The Great Depression* that merits our attention. Before presenting some of the possible lessons for today, we may note that the term "recession" was not in general use at the time that Robbins wrote. Rather, the business cycle consisted of alternations of "prosperity" and "depression." Although since the 1930s we have not experienced a downturn of the magnitude that Robbins described, many parallels can be drawn, at least roughly and usefully.

Robbins reports that the depression that started in 1929 "dwarfed all preceding movements of a similar nature" both in magnitude and intensity. But the precipitating events—notably the stock market crash in the United States and the failure of the Credit-Anstalt Bank in Austria—he tells us, were not bolts out of the blue. Nor does he absolve Great Britain from serious blame. Robbins labels his country's abandonment of the gold standard during this period as "a catastrophe of the first order of magnitude." The author then traces the origin of the Great Depression to the dislocations of "The Great War" (World War I) and the speculative activity that followed the achievement of peace.

As for the fundamental causes of the Great Depression, Robbins states that money is the one thing common to all economic activity in the modern world. In that spirit he points ironically to the cooperation among the major monetary authorities, such as the Bank of England and the U.S. Federal Reserve System. He blames especially the Fed for the excessive monetary ease, designed to avert recession in Great Britain, but which also generated the unsustainable boom conditions in financial markets. The boom, in his view, was bound to be followed by an extended depression.

Robbins attributes the severity of the depression to forces that reduced the flexibility of the economic system. His concerns cover a broad terrain, ranging from the great combinations of industrial firms to the rigidity of labor markets brought about by collective bargaining.

This combination "was a dish of eggs not easy to unscramble." Robbins draws on what he calls orthodox economics, including "the heritage of generations of subtle and disinterested thought." Nevertheless, it may not be too wide off the mark to state that this portion of the book has held up least well over the years. To be fair, we should note the continued inability of the economic profession to develop a fully satisfactory explanation of the complex array of actions and responses that constituted the Great Depression.

As recently as the June 2008 issue of *The Journal of Economic Literature*, Harold Cole of the University of Pennsylvania lamented the "fragmentary state" of economics with respect to the Great Depression. That distinguished economist reminded us all of the challenges that are still faced in developing a truly satisfactory quantitative theory of what happened during the Great Depression.

In that same spirit, Robbins cautioned the reader that no one analysis of the Great Depression is capable of "explaining all its different aspects." In his view, political accidents, deliberate policies, structured weaknesses, and local psychology all played a part. Moreover, as the situation deteriorated, a vicious circle set in. Fear of the future set in motion forces, which brought about the adverse situation envisioned by the worriers.

Robbins also evokes a theme that he repeatedly turns to: the data available at the time to analyze economic developments lack "statistical purity." However, he finds the contemporary numbers adequate to measure "general directions of movement." This is reminiscent of a debate among economists in a more recent period concerning "measurement without theory" and "theory without measurement."

Many of the details of the Great Depression of the 1930s, although different from today's situation, do sound somewhat familiar. Robbins, for example, notes that the fall in the yield of bonds encouraged "the more adventurous spirits" to look elsewhere for higher returns on their investments. This attitude leads to extensive speculation in real estate and to increases in the prices of raw materials. Under such circumstances, more money will be borrowed from the banks to finance speculative operations. The wave of optimism may extend the boom for some time, but "it cannot go on ... the end is certain." The strikingly close parallel with more recent experience is hard to ignore. As Robbins notes, "It was not old-fashioned practice but new-fashioned theory which was responsible for the excesses of the American disaster." The great British economist surely did not mince words, and he went on to criticize sharply the policies of his home country.

Some undesirable side effects of economic activity apparently are quite readily predictable. Robbins explains in plain and forceful prose that the boom preceding the Great Depression provided a favorable atmosphere for the "fraudulent operations of sharks and swindlers." It is when money is easy and profits seem to be there for the taking, that everyone is anxious to be in "a little earlier than his neighbors." Robbins quotes Pope:

> Blest paper credit! Last and best supply!
> That lends corruption lighter wings to fly.

More specifically, the recent manipulations in the sub-marginal mortgage market come to mind when Robbins writes that "the vast mechanism of the operation of high finance," including "a menagerie of tame statisticians" justified the suspension of the traditional maxims of prudence. The prior boom had been remarkable for a change in the methods of straightforward financing. Thus, the experience of the farm sector in the 1930s does sound strikingly familiar to the housing depression of the early twenty-first century: farmers who had mortgaged their farms to expand operations in the boom times of the 1920s found it difficult to meet their financial obligations when economic conditions subsequently softened.

Following the orthodox approach, which is now out of fashion, Robbins chastised the Fed for making credit too easy, citing the numerous reductions in the discount rate and its open market sales of Treasury securities. Supposedly, these actions arrested the protracted liquidation, which Robbins considered to be a basic part of the recovery process. This approach, reminiscent of the public positions of President Herbert Hoover's Secretary of the Treasury, Andrew Mellon, contrasts sharply with the current explanation for the severity of the Depression of the 1930s. Modern economic analysis focuses on the failure of the Fed to expand the money supply in the face of very serious deflationary forces. In any event, the reader should recall that this extensive analysis of the Great Depression was completed in June 1934, several years before that unusual business cycle was concluded.

Robbins also notes that economic downturns are propitious times for the proponents of protectionist restrictions on international commerce. He specifically warns that it is too easy to believe that curtailing imports by means of government restrictions on trade will not result in comparable actions by other countries reducing their imports from the nation initiating the protectionist actions. Robbins connects the enactment of the egregious Smoot-Hawley Tariff in the United States to the simultaneous reduction of foreign lending by American banks. The untimely combination of these two very separate actions exacerbated the economic difficulties facing many other nations. They found it increasingly difficult to obtain funds either by selling goods overseas or obtaining foreign credit—and subsequently reduced their imports from abroad.

As Robbins describes the matter in stern peda-
gogical terms: there occurred on a large scale "the
odd spectacle of the nations of the world zealously
endeavoring to bring about a further contraction
by excluding each other's products." This was a
time when some of the author's contemporaries
were attracted by the siren call of protectionism
(he notes in passing that even John Maynard
Keynes succumbed to that view for a while). Robbins also explained the benefits of open and free
trade in the context of a world beset by high unemployment and slow growth.

Robbins was no narrow specialist, but covers a
wide terrain in this book. Thus, he takes a sar-
castic swipe at the anti-Semitic positions of Adolf
Hitler: "Perhaps inflation is only conceived to be
possible when there are Jews about. When there
are good Aryans behind the counter prices do not
rise!"

His criticism of Franklin D. Roosevelt's New
Deal brings to mind contemporary shortcomings
in government policy. Robbins bluntly states, "…
it had been easier to bamboozle a president than
to debamboozle him." He then notes, in a lower
key, that the various economic measures that the
Roosevelt Administration had introduced "work
in such different directions."

His analysis of the inconsistencies in FDR's farm
policies are biting and also read as if, with minor
editing, they could serve as a relevant criticism of
today's agricultural subsidies. Robbins' criticisms
of U.S. agricultural policies for the 1930s, sadly,
have a very contemporaneous ring: "… it is surely
not irrelevant to point out that an association of
producers with statutory powers to exclude com-

petition is not necessarily the best judge of the interest of consumers."

Robbins also presents an especially pithy criticism of the efforts to expand the scope of governmental planning: ".... 'planning'—ah! magic word—who would not *plan*?" He goes on to point out that the authorities of a planned society would attempt to manage production as a whole "as the general staff manages an army at war." In this area, Robbins presages the future writings of Friedrich Hayek, especially his *Road to Serfdom*. (In scholarly fashion, Robbins cites the work of Ludwig von Mises in the original German; an English translation was not then available.)

Robbins also analyzes the complex relations between the state and the free market. He points out that the emphasis on private property and private risk-taking "in no way" involves the denial of the economic functions of government. After all, as Robbins reminds the reader, private property is itself a creation of the State. Thus, as he warns us, delineating the line between marketplace decision-making and government policymaking is a task of "the utmost complexity, which can only be performed by the State."

Robbins, however, is no aloof economic theorist. He writes about the millions of people to whom "a slice of bacon more or less" still matters. However, he takes what many consider to be a hard line on the question of wage flexibility. He repeatedly warns that attempting to maintain wages at above-market levels will generate increases in unemployment. On reflection, the contemporary debate on the issue of employer-financed fringe benefits demonstrates that the subject of rigidity in payments to workers may be obscured, but it is still very much with us. Thus, current management efforts to increase employee shares of the cost of health insurance benefits can be seen as essentially an updating of Robbins' concern: if wages are not realistically flexible downward, then other parts of the labor compensation package become a center of attention.

Robbins demonstrates his attachment to then conventional thinking by his repeated urgings to return to the gold standard (a topic of discussion that now is limited to a very small minority of "gold bugs"). Indeed, Robbins is steadfast in defending his attachment to gold. When some of his contemporaries blame the gold standard for the difficulties facing the international economy, he responds that the real shortcoming was in not setting the price of gold at the correct level!

In passing, it is fascinating to note how many of the outstanding economists in Robbins' time were also devoting much of their attention, not just to traditional academic concerns, but to the pressing issues of the day. He draws on the contemporary policy writings of Friedrich Hayek, Nicholas Kaldor, John Maynard Keynes, Oscar Morgenstern, and Jacob Viner, all of whom were simultaneously making important contributions to the scholarly literature.

Comparing the statistical work embodied in *The Great Depression* with the current battery of economic data readily available for contemporary analysis is quite illuminating—and ultimately heartening. Robbins laments how difficult it was to compile an index of world expansion. Lacking today's comprehensive data on economic growth for the globe as well as for individual countries, he had to content himself with banking statistics for selected individual nations. Perhaps that also accounts for a major shortcoming in the book (which Robbins much later acknowledged): the lack of macroeconomic analysis as developed by his contemporary Keynes (and his disciples) and subsequently by the path-breaking monetary economist Milton Friedman and his followers.

A word of caution to the reader: despite its fascination to anyone with an appetite for economic history, *The Great Depression* truly is a period piece. Many of the sections are mainly useful in revealing the thinking that pervaded economic circles in the 1930s: for example, the widespread preoccupation with the desire to return to the gold standard. Then again, some of the analysis in the book would have been especially relevant to contemporary U.S. monetary policy officials. That is especially the case of those economists who were so concerned with the prospects for deflation at the beginning of the twenty-first century that they developed a monetary policy easy enough to yield negative real interest rates (interest rates below the inflation rate). Robbins astutely warned that, when productivity is increasing, we should expect prices to fall in the absence of general inflationary forces.

Quite a few of Robbins' observations continue to be relevant today. His criticism of the inefficiency of government institutions surely has contemporary resonance. He notes especially the inability of legislatures to enact laws that do not need to be revised within "twelve months of their being placed on the statute book." This accurately describes the continuing situation in the case of almost any substantial federal legislation. Especially in the case of a major tax law, a technical corrections bill is anticipated within a year! Robbins concludes that the shortcomings of government do not primarily reflect inadequate procedures or techniques. Rather, they result from assuming responsibility for more than they can properly supervise.

Some of the concluding sections of *The Great Depression* have a modern ring to them, albeit sadly. Robbins notes, in connection with the then contemporaneous rise of the Nazi movement, that we now have to live with people whose conceptions of the true ends of life are fundamentally different from our own. He goes on to describe people to whom "the kindly virtues of peace" are contemptible and for whom the destruction of life is a better thing than its preservation. That thought does have a very contemporary flavor in the context of international terrorism. After struggling with the ways of responding to the challenge of totalitarianism, Robbins concludes with the admittedly optimistic conclusion that we are not justified in believing that "reason and persuasion have reached the limits of their effectiveness."

One possibly helpful and upbeat finding of Robbins: when the boom is over, "dislocations and disproportionalities" exist in the world of industry, which changes in monetary policy are not likely to remove. In this "wreckage of false expectations," opportunities may arise for the savvy investor.

In passages foreshadowing a famous statement of Keynes about the power of the academic scribbler, Robbins writes that the ideas which, for good or for bad, have come to dominate policy are the ideas that have been put forward "... by isolated thinkers"; although ideas may be unimportant and ineffective in the short run, "in the long run they can rule the world."

Murray Weidenbaum[1]

Note

1. Murray Weidenbaum holds the Mallinckrodt Distinguished University Professorship at Washington University in St. Louis, where he also serves as honorary chairman of the Weidenbaum Center on the Economy, Government, and Public Policy.

PREFACE

THE following pages make no claim to present an exhaustive account of the events with which they deal. Nor do they set out in full rigour the various analytical theorems upon which they are based. They are merely an attempt, with the aid of what is sometimes called "orthodox" economics, to furnish a succinct commentary on the more conspicuous features of the slump and its antecedents. In doing this I have been most acutely aware of the difficulties of the task I have undertaken. The subject is highly controversial, and many of the conclusions to which I have been led run counter to opinions which have been widely held, at any rate in this country. I put them forward, not with any confidence whatever in the superiority of my own judgment, but in the belief that the point of view from which they spring, which is not specifically my own but is the heritage of generations of subtle and disinterested thought, is a point of view whose applicability to the interpretation of the bewildering problems with which we are now confronted has not as yet been sufficiently recognised.

I have to acknowledge indebtedness to the various friends who have been kind enough to favour me with the benefit of their advice and criticism. My main debt, however, is to Mr. Stanley Tucker, Rockefeller Research Assistant in the Department of Economics, without whose loyal and unremitting labours in the preparation of the charts and the statistical appendix publication at this stage would have been impossible.

LIONEL ROBBINS

THE LONDON SCHOOL OF ECONOMICS
June 1934

CHAPTER I

1914–1933

1. THE object of this Essay is to examine the nature and the causes of the present depression of trade. Its first task, therefore, is to trace the background of the depression and the broad conditions amid which it was generated.

To do this it is necessary to draw the picture on a canvas wider than that which would at first sight seem appropriate to an enterprise of this nature. The onset of the present crisis may perhaps be dated from the autumn of 1929. But its causes and the conditions under which they have operated take their rise long before this date. The body-economic, equally with the body-politic, has been in a state of violent tension ever since the war. We live, not in the fourth, but in the nineteenth, year of the world crisis. If our discussion of the events since 1929 is not to be wholly unrelated to their most significant causes, it must take some account, however brief, of events before that date. 1914 is the beginning of our epoch.

2. For the hundred years which preceded the outbreak of the Great War, the economic system had not at any time shown itself to be in serious danger of grave breakdown. It was a period of unprecedented change. The external conditions of economic activity were in process of continual alteration. In the old world

the advent of steam and machinery was changing
the nature and the structure of manufacturing industry. In the new, the coming of new modes of transport was opening up vast areas, hitherto undeveloped,
both as sources of food supply and raw materials, and
as markets for the products of the manufacturing pro-
cesses. The population of the world, whose normal
state there is reason to suppose to have been more or
less stationary, was growing rapidly. The aggregation
of people into large cities, dependent for the most
elementary necessities of life upon supplies produced
at the other ends of the earth, proceeded at a rate unknown in any earlier epoch. Yet the economic mechanism was adjusted to this complex of change without
anything like the present dislocations, and, year in,
year out, turned out what, for a substantial proportion
of the increasing population, has been regarded as the
basis of an increasing standard of real income. According to the calculations of Sir Josiah Stamp, the level
of real incomes in Great Britain in the years before
the war was four times as great as in the Napoleonic
period.

To say all this is not in the least to contend that the
pre-war period was immune from economic difficulties,
or that what has come since is to be regarded as
spontaneous catastrophe, having no intimate connection with anything that went before. No student of
those times is likely to be unaware of the ups and
downs of trade, the recurrent waves of business depression and unemployment, which ruffle the lines of
secular development. Nor will he be blind to the
increase towards the end of the period in political
tendencies which, viewed in the light of more recent
developments, can be seen to have been fraught with

danger to the stability of the whole system. The Great War itself was the product, not of accident, but of some of these tendencies. Nevertheless, compared with what has come since, the difficulties of those times must be admitted as being of a minor order. During the years for which we have records, the number of unemployed trade-unionists in Great Britain only once rose above 10 per cent. The crises were not such as to disrupt the unity of monetary conditions in the important financial centres. The interventionist and restrictive tendencies of economic policy, although no doubt calculated to retard the increase of productivity, were never such as seriously to threaten to reverse it. There is no need to present the world before the war as a Utopia to point the contrast with what has come after.

3. Into this world there came the catastrophe of war. There is no need at this point to dwell on the intellectual and cultural changes which this catastrophe involved, although for those who are not dominated by a purely materialist conception of history it is arguable that, even in this context, these were the most important changes of all. More germane, however, to the purpose of this survey, are certain more tangible influences.

As an influence on economic activity, the war, and the political changes which followed the war, must be regarded as a vast series of shifts in the fundamental conditions of demand and supply, to which economic activity must be adapted. The needs of war called a huge apparatus of mechanical equipment into being. The resumption of peace rendered it in large part superfluous. The fact of war involved a disruption of the world market. The settlement, which came after, created conditions which aggravated this disruption.

The struggle which was to end nationalist friction in fact gave nationalism new scope.

As an influence on subsequent developments, these changes have a double significance. In the first place, they were discontinuous. They therefore involved vast destruction of capital. Secondly, they were restrictive of free economic activity. They therefore involved a reduction in the productivity of the factors of production. For four years, the capital resources of the belligerent countries of the world were devoted to providing offerings to Mars, which either perished in the moment of their production or remained as useless as the pyramids of the Pharaohs, once the occasion for the sacrifice had ceased. The disruption of the world market, consequent on the war and on the peace settlement, meant a restriction of the area within which the division of labour had scope. It meant therefore a limitation of the increase of wealth to which division of labour gives rise.

Concurrently with these structural dislocations, there came a further series of changes no less important in the causation of post-war difficulties. At the same time as the using up of capital and the lowering of productivity were producing conditions demanding readjustment on a scale hitherto unknown in economic history, the economic system was losing its capacity for adaptation. The successful prosecution of war involved, as we have seen, a large and discontinuous alteration of the "set" of the apparatus of production. This alteration was carried through. But the measures which were necessary to bring it about—the centralisation of control of industrial operations—were such as permanently to impair its capacity for further change. The grouping of industrial concerns into great combinations, the authoritarian fixing of wages and prices, the imposition of the habits of collective bargaining, were no doubt measures which would be justified by appeal to the necessities of war. But they carried with them a weakening of the permanent flexibility of the system, whose effects it is difficult to over-estimate. This was a dish of eggs not easy to unscramble.

Here, as with other contrasts between pre-war and post-war conditions, it is important not to exaggerate differences. It is not contended that the pre-war system was entirely flexible, or that the post-war system has shown itself to be incapable of some adaptation. This would be untrue. All that is argued is that the changes introduced by way of groupings which made for cartellisation on the one hand and a greatly increased rigidity of the labour market on the other, were such as to produce an important and far-reaching impairment of what degree of flexibility there was. In the light of well-known facts regarding the rigidity of wages and the prices of cartellised products in the post-war period, this does not seem to be a contention which is open to serious question.

Beyond all this came the break-up of international monetary unity. For forty years before the war, the financial systems of the leading countries of the world had been linked together by the international Gold Standard. For a century, the Gold Standard had been virtually effective. Trade between different national areas took place on the basis of rates of exchange which fluctuated only between very narrow limits. Capital moved from one part of the world to another, if not with the same ease with which it moved within national areas, at least with much the same effects as regards the volume of credit available. The prices of internationally traded commodities moved together in all the important centres. The price and cost structures of the different financial areas maintained a relationship which was seldom seriously out of equilibrium.

The war put an end to all this. Within a few days of the outbreak of hostilities, in each of the belligerent financial centres, measures had been taken which amounted to an actual, if not to a legally acknowledged, abandonment of the Gold Standard. Of the chief financial centres, the United States was the only one to remain on gold. The others not only suspended the rights of effective convertibility; they each, in greater or lesser degree, resorted to the device of inflation as a means of financing the war. The results were as might have been expected. The gold supplies of the world tended more and more to be concentrated in the vaults of the Federal Reserve Banks. Prices rose in the inflating countries in various degrees, according to the measure of the inflation. In the markets for foreign exchange the conditions of supply and demand reflected the internal depreciation. It was the first phase of a period of international disequilibrium from which we have not yet emerged.

4. The conclusion of peace brought no end to this disorder. The inordinate claims of the victors, the crass financial incapacity of the vanquished, the utter budgetary disorder which everywhere in the belligerent countries was the legacy of the policies pursued during the war, led to a further period of monetary chaos. In the United States a brief inflationary boom was followed by collapse, and then a fairly rapid recovery. In Great Britain the boom and the collapse had no such fortunate sequel: a long period of relative stagnation followed. In continental Europe, the confusion was

without precedent. It was the era of the great inflations. The rouble, the crown and the mark all suffered what was virtually an annihilation of value. The franc and the lira underwent serious depreciation. The results were what was to be expected—severe curtailment of trade, further structural dislocations, capital consumption and the wiping-out of middle-class resources, a further disruption of the basis of the international equilibrium of prices.

5. By the middle of the 'twenties, this intense disorder had come to an end. One by one, budgets were balanced and disordered currencies were restored to some kind of stability. In the spring of 1925, Great Britain and the British dominions returned to the Gold Standard. By the end of the year, of the important countries, only France was still on a fluctuating standard.

There followed a period of good trade—a period, indeed, which in the light of more complete knowledge of the relevant statistics can be seen to have been, for some parts of the world, one of the biggest booms in economic history. Trade revived, incomes rose. Production went ahead by leaps and bounds. International investment was resumed on a scale surpassing even pre-war dimensions. The stock exchanges of the more prosperous centres displayed such strength that speculation for a rise seemed a more certain path to a secure income than all the devices of ancient prudence. It was a period in which the finance ministers of the world, looking forward to years of increasing revenue, felt no hesitation in incurring fresh obligations on the side of expenditure. Men of the type of the late Ivar Kreuger moved rapidly from one capital city to another, arranging without fuss or inconvenience to anybody, what were described as "good constructive loans"—the acolytes of the "new economics". It was in these days that it was said that the trade cycle had become extinct.

Nevertheless, there were certain features of this phase which were such as to distinguish it, if not in kind, at any rate in degree, from other periods of expanding trade. It was pre-eminently an industrial boom. The rise in profitability was essentially a feature of manufacture and raw material producing industry. Throughout the period, the profitability of certain lines of food production was relatively low. In the United States—then as now the centre of the world fluctuation—side by side with extreme prosperity in the manufacturing industries, there existed severe difficulties, and in parts even distress, among the producers of agricultural products. All over the world the relative decline of agriculture was giving rise to severe political strain and desperate attempts, in the shape of pools and restriction schemes, to evade the consequences of technical progress.

Moreover, even in manufacturing industry the boom was not universal. Important areas of manufacturing production experienced its influence only indirectly. Throughout the boom years in the United States, industrial activity anywhere in Great Britain could never have been described as more than moderately good. There were large areas in the North where this description would have been an exaggeration. In Central Europe, particularly in Austria, partly as a result of the peace settlement, partly as a result of internal policy, there was definitely discernible a tendency to capital consumption. In Germany, the appalling shortage of capital created by the war and the post-war inflation was partly compensated by large imports of capital. But the business situation was never normal, and at a much earlier date than elsewhere it became quite obviously perilous.

At the same time, in the financial centres of the world there existed conditions wholly without parallel in any earlier period of prosperity. The stabilisation of European currencies and the fixing of new parities, after the colossal fluctuations of the post-war years, had been carried through on the basis of what very often could only be described as hit-or-miss methods; and although in some cases the miss was not very great, in others it was considerable. In the case of Great Britain, the parity chosen was almost certainly too high. In France there is reason to suppose that the error was in the opposite direction. The result was a most peculiar state of inter-local monetary disequilibrium. The centres which had returned too high were continually in danger of losing gold; the centres which had returned too low were almost embarrassed by the gold they attracted. Now it so happened that the centre which suffered chiefly from over-valuation was also the chief centre of organised capital export. While the over-valued exchanges made long-term capital export from London a highly difficult operation, the relatively high rates, which were necessary to keep gold from flowing out, were especially tempting to short-term balances. Hence, throughout the whole of this period there existed in one of the chief financial centres of the world a lack of balance between long- and short-term investment which was itself conducive to disequilibrium and latent with dangers of extensive catastrophe, should anything occur to disturb the insecure prosperity elsewhere.

6. Thus, in spite of the appearance of considerable prosperity and a very real measure of revival of trade and industry, the period immediately preceding the slump was not without conditions which might justifiably have given rise to very grave anxiety. Clearly, if the forces making for prosperity were to slacken, the ensuing depression was likely to be a depression of more than usual severity.

They did slacken. Looking back, it is possible to discern the beginning of the depression about the end of 1928, when the flow of American lending to Germany first began to lose its pace. By the middle of 1929, the evidences of serious weakening in that part of the world were unmistakeable. In certain raw material producing centres, too, there were signs of weakness quite early in the summer.

But the main tide of American speculation continued to flow with undiminished strength until the autumn. As early as February the authorities of the Federal Reserve System had become persuaded that the boom had reached such dimensions that a crash was inevitable. But, in spite of private warnings, rising discount rates, and all kinds of unofficial indications, the rise of stock exchange values continued. Then suddenly there came a crack. The collapse of the Hatry swindles in London caused a sudden tightening of markets there. The rate of interest was advanced to $6\frac{1}{2}$ per cent. In New York there was a sympathetic movement. On October 23rd the Dow-Jones index of the price of industrial shares in New York dropped about 21 points ; during the next six days it fell about 76 points more. Prosperity was at an end. The bottom had dropped out of the market.

7. The depression which followed has dwarfed all

preceding movements of a similar nature both in magnitude and in intensity. In 1929 in the United States the index of security prices stood in the neighbourhood of 200-210. In 1932 it had fallen to 30-40. Commodity prices in general fell in the same period by 30 to 40 per cent; the fall in particular commodity markets was even more catastrophic. Production in the chief manufacturing countries of the world shrank by anything from 30 to 50 per cent: and the value of world trade in 1932 was only a third of what it was three years before. It has been calculated by the International Labour Office that in 1933, in the world at large, something like 30 million persons were out of work.[1] There have been many depressions in modern economic history but it is safe to say that there has never been anything to compare with this. 1929 to 1933 are the years of the Great Depression.

[1] For more extensive statistical information see Tables 1 to 12, Statistical Appendix.

CHAPTER II

1. WHY did these things happen?

Before proceeding to a tentative explanation, there are certain misconceptions which demand our attention both on account of their widespread acceptation and their possible influence on policy. Incidentally their examination will bring to light certain matters which have an important bearing on the explanations eventually to be offered.

2. Perhaps the most conspicuous feature of the statistics which we have just cited is the fall of commodity prices. A fall of 40 per cent in gold prices in four years is an event without precedent. In popular discussion, people often speak as if this were, not only a symptom, but actually the cause of the slump and its various attendant difficulties. The fall of prices is the cause of the depression, they urge.

Such a view is based upon misapprehension. There can be no doubt that when prices fall as rapidly and as severely as they have done in this depression all sorts of difficulties, which would not otherwise have existed, necessarily come into being. The increasing budgetary deficits and the growing weight of fixed indebtedness of which so much has been heard in the past few years, are difficulties of this kind. These difficulties may rightly be described as consequences of the

12

fall of prices. But it does not in the least follow that the fall of prices is, in any sense, a prime cause of the depression. Indeed, if we reflect upon the rôle played by prices in the markets in which prices arise, such a conclusion must at once be seen to be fallacious. In the market, prices are the resultant of the forces underlying, on the one hand, commodity supply, and on the other, money demand. A fall of prices does not occur spontaneously. It occurs only as a result of changes in one or other of these factors. No doubt when it occurs, it may bring with it the further complications we have noticed. But its occurrence is not the cause—it is the effect—of the fundamental fluctuation. In the search for ultimate causes it constitutes the problem, not the solution.

3. It follows, therefore, that any explanation of the slump which is to escape the charge of complete superficiality must go behind prices to the causes of which prices are the resultant. That is to say, it must look either to commodity supply or to demand expressed in terms of money.

It is in this sense, if we are to do justice to them at all, that we must interpret those theories which explain the slump in terms of over-production. So long as there remain anywhere wants which are unsatisfied, it is quite clear that there cannot be over-production in the sense of a real superfluity of commodities. No doubt, as against those who wish to cure depression by all-round restriction, it is important to reiterate this homely truth. But the over-production which is invoked in popular explanations of the depression is not over-production in this sense. It is merely over-production in the sense that, in wide groups of important markets, at the price prevailing, the supply cannot be sold at a profit. Against appeal to this unquestion-able fact it is absurd to brandish the platitude that even in the best of times many wants are left un-satisfied.

Now there can be no doubt that in the present de-pression, and indeed in every depression of which we have knowledge, over-production in this sense has been present. The fall in profitability in many lines of in-dustry due to changed relations, or anticipations of changed relations, between supply and demand is one of the most conspicuous features of the beginning of all downward fluctuations of this nature. It is a move-ment which often shows itself in the index of security prices long before commodity prices have been affected. The appeal to over-production of this sort therefore has a solid basis of fact.

But here, as with the appeal to the fall in commodity prices, the alleged explanation proves to be nothing but another way of putting the fundamental problem. Over-production in this sense exists. But why does it exist? Why is it that supply exceeds demand in so many *different* markets?

It is useful to put the question thus, for in this way the real nature of the problem—the simultaneity of over-production in many lines of industry—is especially emphasised. Over-production in one line of industry only is not likely to lead to general depression. If the industry is one from which producers cannot shift, consumers get the larger supply at cheaper prices and the producers have to put up with lower incomes. If migration into other lines of industry is possible, then supply is restricted by a redistribution of labour and capital. In a competitive system, the fact that, in one line of industry, costs are above prices, definitely implies that the different factors, whose prices go to make up cost here, would produce elsewhere a more valuable product. In either case, the disturbances involved are not of the sort which is necessarily conducive to general disequilibrium.

It is sometimes thought that an increase of production which leads to lower prices and lower incomes in a particular branch of industry is detrimental to production elsewhere, in that it involves a diminution in the demand for the products of other industries. An increase of agricultural production, it is held, leads to a fall in agricultural prices, and this, in turn, implies a diminution in demand for the products of manufacturing industry—a diminution of purchasing power. Such a view undoubtedly underlies the agrarian policy at present being pursued in the United States. It is sometimes said that the growing cheapness of agricultural products is detrimental to the prosperity of manufacturing production in Great Britain.

This belief is misleading. Let us suppose that, owing to technical progress, the supply of wheat increases. Let us suppose further that, owing to the relatively inelastic nature of the demand for wheat, the price of wheat falls more than proportionately, and the producers of wheat have therefore lower incomes. Does this mean that that much purchasing power will have disappeared from the world? Not at all. It is true that the wheat producers will have less to spend. But the consumers, who now get more wheat for a smaller outlay, will have more money left over. It may very well be that they will not spend this increase on exactly the same things that the wheat producers would have purchased. But they will be in a position to buy more of something; and this will render any reshuffling of the labour force which the changed direction of demand makes necessary, a comparatively easy process.

But is it not possible that the money thus transferred may not be spent at all—that the consumers of wheat, having obtained their wheat for less, hoard the difference rather than spend it? In such a case, no doubt, there would be a net diminution of spending and the over-production in one industry would have injurious effects, *via* the hoarding process, on others. But is such a state of affairs likely, if the initial over-production takes place in only one industry? Why should consumers hoard? Why should they not spend more on something else? The possibility of hoarding of this sort must not be ruled out altogether. But so long as the initial increase in production is confined to one industry it seems, *prima facie*, improbable. Only if there is a fall of prices due to a simultaneous over-production in many lines of industry does such a tendency seem at all probable.

But this brings us back to the real problem. Why do such simultaneous changes take place? Why is there over-production in many lines of industry?

4. Considerations of this sort have led many to the belief that the ultimate cause of this, and indeed of all other depressions, is to be looked for, not on the side of commodity supply, but rather on the side of money. Money is the one thing common to almost all economic activity in the modern world. Is it not probable that disturbances affecting many lines of industry at once will be found to have monetary causes?

The suggestion is plausible and, as we shall eventually see, it is probable that it contains an important core of truth. But the kinds of monetary explanation are various and need separate examination.

Perhaps the most widely held view of this sort is that which attributes the slump to deflation. A fall of prices so great as the fall we have recently witnessed cannot be wholly due to increased technical productivity. Clearly there must be a strong element of monetary causation involved. The slump, therefore, is due to deflation. Such is the most popular monetary explanation of our present difficulties. It is not difficult to see what implications are held to follow as regards the policy appropriate to recovery.

Unfortunately, there seems to be no reason to regard this explanation as sufficient. If we take deflation to mean a deliberate curtailment of the supply of money, there seems to be no evidence of its existence on a large scale either before or since the slump commenced. Before the slump, if we take the world as a whole, all the evidence shows that the supply of money in the widest sense was expanding very rapidly. Since the slump, Central Banks and Governments have vied with each other in promoting policies calculated to bring about easy money conditions. Save perhaps in Germany, where the exigencies of the transfer problem compelled a certain stringency of credit, there is no evidence of deflation, in the sense of a deliberate restriction of credit. The following chart,[1] which shows the effects of the "open market" policy of the Federal Reserve System and the Bank of England, should be a sufficient refutation of the charge that the Central Banks of the world have deliberately brought about deflation.

If, however, we take deflation to mean, not merely a deliberate curtailment by Central Banks of the supply

[1] For the statistics upon which it is based, see Tables 13 and 14 of the Appendix.

of money, but a slowing up of the frequency with
which money is used by different members of the com-

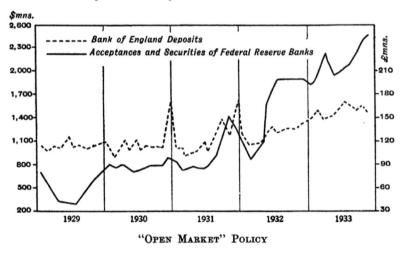

"OPEN MARKET" POLICY

munity, then there can be no possible question of its
existence in the years since the slump. The figures of
bank debits divided by bank deposits give a rough
idea of the average rapidity with which money is
changing hands. The following chart shows the extra-

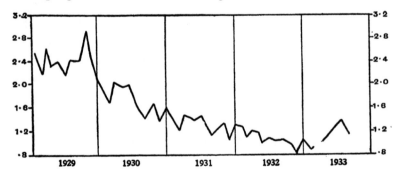

UNITED STATES—VELOCITY OF CIRCULATION OF BANK DEPOSITS

ordinary diminution which has taken place in the
United States since the slump began.[1]

[1] See Statistical Appendix, Table 15.

There can thus be no denying the existence of deflation in this sense in this period. But here, as in the case of all the theories we have so far examined, the diagnosis reveals, not a solution, but a problem. Why was there deflation in this sense? Why did people tend to leave money on idle deposit, rather than invest it in active business? Surely we cannot regard such a phenomenon as a spontaneous evil. Under capitalism there are permanent influences tending in the opposite direction. Under capitalism he who hoards is punished —punished by the loss of interest. If therefore people incur this punishment we are entitled to assume that something has gone wrong—that some other disturbance is the prior cause of the depression. To appeal to deflation as an ultimate explanation is only one degree less superficial than to appeal to the mere fact of the fall in prices. A monetary explanation which is to command respect must show why deflation takes place at all.

5. It is sometimes thought that the coming of depression is due to a shortage of gold. In order that business may remain stable it is said it is necessary that prices should not fall. In order that prices should not fall it is necessary that the gold supply should increase so as to keep pace with advancing productivity. The failure of prices to remain stable is therefore due to a deficiency of gold.

It is clear that a theory of this sort cannot be dismissed as a mere restatement of the problem. If it were true that it is necessary for prices to remain stable for business to continue to be profitable; if it were true that for prices to remain stable it is necessary for the gold supply to increase by a certain percentage every year; if it were true that during the period leading up to

the depression the gold supply had failed to conform
to these requirements, then clearly here would be a
genuinely causal explanation of our troubles. Unfortunately none of these things seem to be true. It is
not difficult to demonstrate this.

Let us take first the proposition that for business
conditions to be profitable it is necessary for the price-
level to be stationary. It is often thought that this
view is generally accepted by economists—that it is
only questioned by a tiny handful of "sadistic deflationists". In fact this is the reverse of the truth.
Whatever their differences on other aspects of monetary theory, the majority of economists of repute in
recent times have held quite definitely the view that
there is nothing detrimental to business stability in a
price-level falling with increased productivity. Mar-
shall, Edgeworth, Taussig, Hawtrey, Robertson, Pigou,
to mention only the names of English-speaking economists, have all been of this opinion.

The reason is very simple. Technical progress—the
main cause of an increase in the volume of production—is essentially a cost-reducing process. Now it
is clear that there is nothing inimical to the profitability of particular undertakings if the prices of the
things they produce fall *pari passu* with their cost.
Why should the mere amalgamation of particular
prices into a statistical average in any way affect the
position?

It is sometimes thought that this argument ignores
the existence of fixed interest charges and similar
obligations. But this is a misapprehension. The argument is that, *if* costs fall, prices can fall too, without
loss of profitability: it is beside the point to say that
some costs do not fall. So far as Government debt is

concerned, it is true that in such circumstances the "real value" of each pound's worth of debt rises. But it is not true that the "real burden" rises. By hypothesis the fall in prices is due to increased productivity. There is a larger product out of which to pay the larger interest. All that happens is that *rentiers* share in the increase of productivity. This may or may not be thought to be ethically desirable. But it imposes no mechanical friction on the smooth working of the economic system. The real burden of debt increases in the way suggested only when the price fall is due, not to increased productivity, but to absolute deflation. Hence there is no foundation for the view that the gold supply must "keep pace" with increased productivity; so long as it "keeps pace" with the increase of population there is no serious ground for fearing a gold shortage.

But let us put these refined considerations aside and concentrate on the facts of the situation we are examining. Even if it were true that, for business to be stable, the gold supply must keep pace with productivity, it would still be untrue that the gold supply actually failed to conform to these requirements in the period under discussion. The rate of increase which is commonly held to be desirable is from $2\frac{1}{2}$ to 3 per cent per annum. There are grave reasons for suspecting the whole basis of the statistical operation by which these results are reached. But for the sake of argument let us accept them. The following table[1] shows the state of the world's monetary stocks of gold for the years 1925–30:

[1] See Annex to the *Final Report* of the Gold Delegation of the League of Nations. The Table was originally published in the *Statistical Yearbook of the League of Nations, 1931–32* (Geneva, 1932).

WORLD'S MONETARY GOLD STOCKS

End of	$ millions.	End of	$ millions.
1925 . .	10,244	1928 . .	10,953
1926 . .	10,496	1929 . .	11,201
1927 . .	10,602	1930 . .	11,715

It will be seen that the monetary gold reserves of the world as a whole increased at a rate of between $2\frac{1}{2}$ and 3 per cent per annum. Even if the theory on which the explanation of the slump in terms of absolute gold shortage is based were correct, it would be inapplicable because it fails to fit the facts. The assertion of a gold shortage is unfounded.

6. Confronted with arguments of this sort, those who are disposed to explain the present difficulties in terms of the vagaries of gold supply usually fall back on another kind of argument. They appeal, not to *shortage*, but to *maldistribution* of the precious metal. They admit that the gold supply as a whole has been sufficient. But they urge that its distribution has been such as to prevent its effective use. There has been too much gold in France and America they say; too little in the rest of the world. For this the banking authorities in the two countries first named are to blame. They have not worked the Gold Standard according to the "rules of the game". They have sterilised their enormous gold reserves. For a time the rest of the world was able to progress in spite of this policy, but eventually the pressure became too great and depression set in. A highly sensational mythology has been embroidered around this argument.

It is important to examine this carefully. It is an argument which has received extraordinarily wide acceptance in Great Britain. It has influenced our views regarding the economic policy of the future. It has caused much international misunderstanding. It has led to much self-righteous denunciation of our neighbours. Yet in fact it is almost completely false.

Let us first be clear about the problem at issue. There can be no doubt that, at the time of the break-up of the International Gold Standard, the gold supplies of the world were distributed in a highly abnormal manner. At the end of June 1931 over 60 per cent of the central gold reserves of the world (apart from the U.S.S.R.) were in two countries: the United States of America and France. There can be no doubt, moreover, that from the time of the break in prosperity in the autumn of 1929, the gold which flowed into these countries did not produce a commensurate expansion of credit. But this is no proof that the slump was the consequence of this movement. On the contrary, there is every reason to suppose that this movement was the consequence of the slump. It is a well-known phenomenon of the trade cycle that, from the turn of trade onwards, the creditor countries tend to receive interest on the money they have lent in the boom in gold rather than in goods. It is well known, too, that during times of depression a reinforcement of the gold reserves of a central bank does not necessarily immediately produce a commensurate increase of borrowing. It is clear that the authorities of the Federal Reserve Bank and the Bank of France did nothing to prevent their increased reserves becoming effective. It is not really sensible, therefore, to attribute what happened after 1929 to their policy; the causes of the gold flows after 1929 are obvious, and though it may rightly be argued that they were aggravated by tariff policies adopted after that date,[1] it is to lose all sense of proportion to regard them as the causes rather than as the consequences of the slump. The real problem relates to what happened before, not after, the depression became intense. Did the French and American authorities transgress the rules of the Gold Standard game in the period before that date?

What are "the rules of the Gold Standard game"?

Broadly speaking they are simply these: that centres receiving gold should expand credit, and centres losing gold should contract credit. In detail, they require that the expansions and contractions should more or less counterbalance each other so that payments between national areas should be on the same footing as payments within national areas; *i.e.* should involve no net expansion or contraction of the money supply in the world as a whole. When the gold supply of the world as a whole is increasing, the situation is more complicated as regards the absolute magnitude of the requirements of expansion and contraction; but the broad principle remains the same as regards flows from one country to another. Inter-local transfers, as such, should involve no net expansion or contraction.

It follows, therefore, that we can judge the validity of the theory we are discussing by examination of the banking statistics of the countries concerned. Were gold imports sterilised or not? That is the question at issue.

Let us first take the United States of America. The following chart shows the movements of gold reserves and effective bank credit in the United States during the period under discussion:[2]

---

[1] It is important to remember that the notorious Hawley Smoot Tariff only became operative in 1930. There were no important alterations in U.S. tariff policy between 1922 and that date.

[2] For the figures on which the chart is based see Statistical Appendix, Tables 16 and 17.

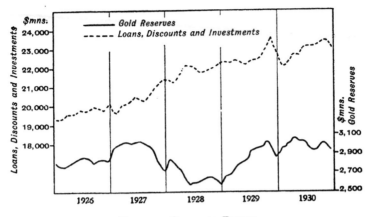

Is this a picture of gold sterilisation? Surely not. It is a picture rather (or part of a picture) of a considerable expansion of credit. (How great this expansion was we shall examine further in the next chapter.) Far from indicating any infringement of the rules of the Gold Standard game in the sense of inadequate expansion, it indicates, if anything, an infringement in the opposite direction. From the spring of 1927 until late in 1928—the period which is regarded by many as decisive for the genesis of the collapse which followed—there was taking place in the United States *an expansion of credit on a declining gold basis*. The Americans are surely not altogether to be blamed when they show some impatience at our interpretation of their policy!

The French position is a little more complex. There is some reason to suppose that the parity at which the Gold Standard was restored in France was, if anything, on the low side. To the extent that this is true it is correct to argue that more gold must have flowed in that direction than would otherwise have been the case. But it does not seem correct to argue that, once there, the gold was deliberately sterilised. The following chart shows the movement of the gold reserves plus foreign assets of the Bank of France and the notes in circulation against it:[1]

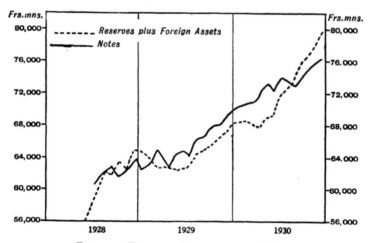

BANK OF FRANCE—RESERVES AND NOTES

There is no obvious "sterilisation" here. As gold flows in or as foreign assets are acquired, so the note issue is enlarged. Nor is there evidence of sterilisation in the accounts of the commercial banks. Owing to an extension of demand for cash the volume of deposits actually sinks during this period, but it sinks proportionately less than the cash reserve. The reserve as a percentage of deposits therefore actually diminishes. The table[2] on the following page shows its movements.

Where this cash went to is a difficult question to determine. There is reason to suppose that some was immobilised in the savings banks. But that much went into active circulation seems to be sufficiently shown by the index of cost of living during that period, which

[1] See Statistical Appendix, Table 18.
[2] See Balogh, "The Import of Gold into France", *Economic Journal*, 1930, p. 447. (Extracted from Jean Loriot, "Les Banques", *Revue d'Économie Politique*, 1930, p. 542.) The whole article is a mine of illuminating information on this difficult question.

RESERVES OF THE CREDIT BANKS AS A PERCENTAGE
OF DEPOSITS

	1927.	1928.	1929.
January	18	20	15
March	27	18	14
June	40	18	14
September	31	16	14
December	23	18	14

rose from 498 in the last quarter of 1927 to 565 in the last quarter of 1929.[1]

There seems no reason, therefore, to accuse either the American or French authorities of deliberate sterilisation of gold during the period under discussion. In both countries there was expansion as gold flowed in. But it may well be asked: Was the expansion sufficient, having regard to what was going on elsewhere? To answer this it is necessary to look at the British statistics.

If we were to believe what is commonly said about British experience during this period we should expect to find a substantial contraction. Moreover if we have regard to the requirements of Gold Standard theory we should entertain similar expectations. For there can be no doubt that during this period Great Britain was out of international equilibrium. Even when we did not actually lose gold we only retained it by all sorts of devices—including, so it is said, occasional appeals *ad misericordiam* to French bankers not to withdraw their balances. The sterling exchange tended continuously to be in the neighbourhood of the gold export point during the greater part of the period we

[1] Paris Commission on Cost of Living.

are discussing. But the figures do not bear out these expectations. The following chart[1] shows the movements of the gold reserve of the Bank of England and the deposits of the London Clearing Banks from 1925 to 1929:

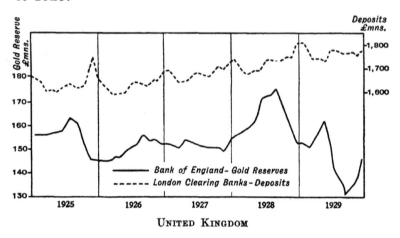

UNITED KINGDOM

Clearly there is no evidence here of deflation. Deposits actually increased from a yearly average of £1623·2 millions in 1925 to £1762·5 millions in 1929. There may have been some offset to this in an increase in the proportion of time deposits to current accounts. But of *deflation*, in any sense of that much abused word, there can be no question.

But this puts a new complexion on the French and American figures. So long as Great Britain, the centre tending to lose gold, was not contracting, the other centres were under no obligation, according to "the rules of the Gold Standard game", to expand. Indeed, in so far as they did so, they were risking a net inflation. As we have seen, in America this risk was taken —with what results we shall see later. In France, as

---

[1] See Tables 19 and 20, Statistical Appendix, and the chart in Chapter V. p. 84.

was only natural in a country which had just emerged from the horrors of a big inflation, the policy was much more cautious. But it is clear that if "the rules of the Gold Standard game" were infringed during these years it was not in France or America.

Moreover—and this is a point which even the apologists of France and America have often over-looked—while Great Britain remained out of equilibrium, it is difficult to see how, in the absence of a complete reversal of existing habits of foreign lending in the case of France, and a drastic change in tariff policy in the case of America, the monetary authorities of these two countries could have avoided receiving gold, save by carrying out a degree of inflation which all the experience of post-war years suggested to be fraught with disaster. A country which is out of international equilibrium—as Great Britain was during this period—acts, as it were, as a watershed of the precious metal. The fact that it is out of equilibrium is the cause of a gold flow to other centres. What maldistribution there was in these years, therefore, is to be ascribed, not to gold sterilisation on the part of America and France—this thesis does not stand examination—but to the state of continued disequilibrium with the rest of the world which was the fate of Great Britain. The theory that the maldistribution of gold in the period 1925 to 1929 caused deflation therefore falls to the ground. In so far as there was maladjustment it caused, not deflation, but inflation. This leads to the thesis which is the subject of the next chapter.

CHAPTER III

THE GENESIS OF THE DEPRESSION

1. So far, the various explanations of the depression which we have examined have all proved to be defective; some because they were not explanations at all but merely restatements of the problem; some because the assumptions on which they rested were in obvious conflict with fact. Where then are we to turn?

2. Let us go back a little to a point which was raised in the last chapter when we were discussing over-production. We saw there that one way of describing the slump was to depict it as a simultaneous breakdown of the profitability of many different lines of industry. It is well known, in fact, that this breakdown is most serious in the industries producing what are known as producers' goods; that is to say, the so-called constructional industries and the industries producing raw materials.[1] In these industries the depression shows itself as a condition of over-production, a condition in which costs are higher than prices, a condition in which the supply coming forward is not taken up at profitable prices, a condition in which the businesses engaged in these lines of industry find that their earlier expectations are not justified by the state of the market, a condition in which earlier errors of anticipation are revealed.

[1] See Tables 8 and 9, Statistical Appendix, for evidence on this point.

One way of putting our problem, therefore, is to ask why the errors thus revealed were originally committed, why they occurred in this peculiar form. It is quite clear that the leaders of business are at no time equipped with perfect foresight. We should always expect some mistakes to be made somewhere. But in the absence of special information we should expect a random distribution. We should not expect this peculiar cluster of errors. Why should the leaders of business in the various industries producing producers' goods make errors of judgement at the same time and in the same direction?

Now it seems probable, as was hinted in the last chapter, that a dislocation which is common to many industries, if it does not actually originate on the side of money, will at least be transmitted and enlarged though the monetary medium. This provides a clue of a kind to the solution of our problem. But it does not, in itself, explain the peculiar distribution of error. Money is spent on everything. Why do not fluctuations in the supply of or the demand for money affect all lines of production equally? Are there any reasons for supposing that monetary changes will bring about the kind of error we are contemplating?

3. Let us first see if such a thing is theoretically conceivable. If this proves to be the case, we can then proceed to discover whether the assumptions on which our theory is based have a counterpart in the reality of the fluctuation we are examining.

Our problem relates to demand expressed in terms of money. It is necessary, therefore, to be quite clear wherein money demand consists.

If we take a cross-section of the industrial system at any moment of time, the activities of supply there discernible fall quite naturally into two groups. On the one hand we have the supply of goods and services ready for immediate consumption—bread, fuel, domestic service, etc. On the other hand we have the supply of things which directly or indirectly contribute chiefly to the consumption of the future. In this group fall raw materials, semi-manufactures, machines, factories, and all those durable consumption-goods like houses whose consumptive uses stretch out over long periods ahead. This division corresponds more or less to the familiar statistical division between consumers' goods and producers' goods save that with the producers' goods we must here include durable consumption-goods such as houses. In conception, this distinction between production for present and future consumption is quite clear and definite. In practice we have to be content with rough classification. A suit of clothes is a durable consumption-good. But we usually class it with consumption-goods. If we like, we may make a distinction between the supply of income-goods and the supply of capital-goods, remembering that the use of a house for which rent is paid will be an income-good and the house itself considered as an object of ownership will be a capital-good.

Corresponding to these activities of supply there will be streams of money demand. On the one hand, there will be streams of money being spent on goods for immediate consumption. On the other hand, business men and others will be spending money on goods and services whose fruits will only be available in the future. The housewife will be spending money on bread, fuel, etc. The baker will be spending money on the labour he employs to make bread, on replenishing his stocks of flour, perhaps on repairing his oven, and

so on and so forth. The distinction here is roughly the
same as the distinction between expenditure out of
income and capital expenditure. The sums of money
spent by consumers, in normal times at any rate, will
be part or the whole of their money-incomes, moneys
which have accrued to them as a result of the labour
which they do as producers or the property which, in
one way or another, they lend out. The business men
will be using their capital—money released by the sale
of stock or new funds borrowed in one way or another
from the capital market. Corresponding to our distinction relating to supply we may distinguish between
the demand for income-goods and the demand for
capital-goods.

The minute circumstances determining expenditure
on income-goods need not concern us here. But the
direction of capital expenditure deserves a little
further attention. As we have seen, at any moment of
time business men must be conceived as spending
money on particular objects—re-investing capital
which has been freed by previous sales, or investing
new sums which they have saved themselves or borrowed from the capital market. What determines the
direction of their expenditure? In the capitalist
system, within the limits prescribed by law, free capital
can be spent on anything. A business man who has
capital free may re-invest it in his business, doing the
same sort of thing he has done before. Or he may put it
elsewhere. What in fact are the considerations govern-
ing the direction of his expenditure?

Clearly in particular instances there may be all sorts
of non-pecuniary considerations. But, speaking broadly,
it is not misleading to say that the main considerations
are anticipations of profit. Money goes where, taking

everything into account, the profits are expected to be highest. The business man considers costs on the one side and prices on the other, and tries to put his money where the margin of profit is greatest. If therefore the return on capital in different lines of industry is not equal (and it never actually becomes equal) there is a tendency for capital to shift from those branches and methods of production where it is relatively lower to those where it is relatively higher. The rate of return on capital is, as it were, the governor of the system.

One further point before we utilise these elementary notions in examining the effects of monetary changes. It should be clear that at any moment there must exist possibilities of production which might be utilised if the profitability of other lines of industry were not so high. When the rate of interest drops from 4 to 3 per cent, a whole range of enterprises, which were not worth while when 4 per cent was the rule, now become attractive. Factories can be built, machines constructed, transport facilities extended, housing provided, which, when the higher rate prevailed, were out of the question. The owners of free capital would not undertake these things themselves if a higher return could be obtained elsewhere. They could not profitably have been undertaken on borrowed money, since the cost of borrowing was too high. The anticipated rate of return on capital, therefore, performs the double function of guiding the direction of existing investment and confining it to enterprise yielding a return above a certain margin.

4. So far we have supposed that money spent at any moment, either by business men or consumers, is money which has been released either by sales of stock, the rendering of services, or the hiring out of

property. We have assumed the total supply of currency and credit to be constant. We have tacitly excluded the possibility of an augmentation of money demand either by way of an increase of currency, or by an increase in the rate at which currency and credit are used. We must now examine what happens if this occurs. We must examine the effects on production of monetary changes.

Let us suppose, for the sake of simplicity, an increase in the supply of money.

Now it is very important, from our point of view, to be clear how this increase actually comes about. Suppose that by a governmental decree all money holdings were to be doubled; that is to say, suppose that all balances at the banks were multiplied by two and all holders of cash were entitled to treat each note and coin in their possession as double its previous face value. In such circumstances, in a free economy with fairly full employment, there is no reason to suppose that great disturbances would follow. The competition of buyers would lead to the fairly quick marking up of all prices to something like double their original level. Some distributive changes there would be as a result of the existence of long-term contracts. *Rentiers* would continue at the old level of income. Profit-makers and possibly wage-earners would benefit correspondingly. These distributive changes would possibly lead to shifts in demand for particular commodities. But there seems no reason to expect that a general oscillation of any importance would be generated.

But, in the real world, new money is not made available in this way. In normal times, expansion and contraction of the money supply comes, not *via* the printing press and government decree, but *via* an expansion of credit through the banks. The rate of discount of the Central Bank is the main regulator of money supply. This involves a mode of diffusion of new money radically different from the case we have just examined—a mode of diffusion which may have important effects on the nature and direction of production. Let us see how this happens.

Let us suppose that, for reasons which for the moment we will leave uninvestigated, the Central Banks of the world make their rates of discount lower than would be justified by the volume of voluntary saving coming into the system. (We shall return later on to a discussion of the possible reasons for such a policy.) What are likely to be the effects on production?

Let us ignore, for the time being, the rather intricate mechanism by which the initial change will transmit itself through the capital market. The fundamental fact on which we must concentrate our attention is that borrowing is cheaper. The structure of interest rates has fallen. This means that the profitability of all forms of production which involve making things which only yield services at a later date, or over a long period of time, is increased. Consider the position of a speculative builder when the rate at which he borrows falls by one per cent, say from 6 per cent to 5. Suppose he has been paying £1000 for a certain collection of materials. Interest on that at 6 per cent is £60. When the rate falls to 5 per cent and the price of existing house property rises accordingly, he will be making an increased profit until the price rises to something a little less than £1200. Clearly it will pay to borrow more.

We can perhaps see this even more clearly if we use the language of the real-estate market. A fall in the rate of interest implies an increase in the number of years' income which it is worth while to pay for the possession of land outright. When the rate of interest is 5 per cent the corresponding number of years' purchase is 20. When it is 4 per cent it is 25. Now this applies not merely to land and houses but to all kinds of capital instruments. The longer-lived the capital instrument, or the greater its distance from consumption, the more its value is affected by the change in the rate of interest. The shorter-lived it is, or the less its distance from consumption, the less is it affected. The value of flour in the baker's shop is hardly affected at all by a cheapening of the cost of borrowing. The value of mines, forests, houses and heavy factory equipment is enormously affected.

It follows, therefore, that the bulk of the new borrowing will be undertaken by those who propose to engage in enterprises of this nature. The new money will flow to those parts of the economic system most affected by the rate of interest. There will be an increased demand for what we have called capital-goods. There will be a boom in the constructional industries and the industries producing raw materials. Producers in these industries, on the strength of the new demands, will be able to bid away from other industries factors of production common to both. The new labour supply will go into these industries rather than elsewhere. Raw materials, such as coal, pig iron and timber, will tend to be used in greater proportions in these parts of the economic system. The production of "producers' goods" and durable consumption-goods, such as houses, will increase.

So far, the phenomena we have described are almost exactly similar to the phenomena we should expect to accompany a fall in the rate of interest which was due to an increase in voluntary saving. But there is this very important difference. An increase in voluntary saving which is made effective in the investment market, means a spontaneous change in the proportion of money spent on income-goods and capital-goods— a change in favour of the latter. It is of the essence of saving that it involves a proportionate slackening of expenditure on present consumption, and a proportionate increase of expenditure on making things which will only be consumable in the future. But the change we have been describing involves a change in the amount spent on capital-goods without any diminution, on the part of the recipients of income, of expenditure on consumption-goods. The business men who have borrowed the new money from the banks compete with the demands which come from those whose money has been secured by the sale of stocks, the performance of work or the hiring out of their property.

But these sums of new money which come from the banks do not remain at the stage of demand for raw materials and the products of the constructional industries. Gradually, as they filter through the economic system, they become ultimate income. Now there is nothing which justifies us in assuming that the recipients of income will necessarily increase the proportion of their incomes that they save. It follows, therefore, that as the new money becomes income we must expect a strengthening of the demand, not for capital-goods, but for income-goods. The old proportion between demand for income-goods and demand for capital-goods tends to be re-established.

But what does this mean in terms of the relative profitability of different lines of industry? Surely that the producers making for immediate consumption will now be in a stronger position to bid against the producers of capital-goods for the factors of production which they use in common and for new loans from the banks. And what does this mean? A tendency to a rise in costs and a hardening of market rates of interest. Wages rise. Interest rates in the short-loan market rise still more. But this means that the anticipations on which the producers of capital-goods planned their extensions of production are frustrated. What do they do? Probably they try to obtain new credits at the banks. For a time this may be possible. The initial prospects of profitability will in all probability have tempted both banks and individuals to reduce their margin of liquidity. But eventually the rise in costs and in the rate of interest becomes too great. The error of the initial anticipations becomes revealed. Investment in the lines of industry most affected by the rate of interest is seen to be unprofitable. The supply of capital-goods coming forward encounters a slackening demand. There ensues depression in the constructional industries and the industries producing raw materials.

5. So much by way of bare essential outline of the manner in which an inflationary extension of credit may generate collective error on the part of the producers of capital-goods. It is not difficult to fill in sufficient detail as regards the actual movement of the capital markets to give the picture a much more familiar appearance.

Let us start, as before, from a state of affairs in which the rate of discount of the Central Banks has moved downwards. We may assume that the Central Banks are in a position to make this rate effective either in virtue of the actual market situation or of "management" in the shape of purchases of securities in the open market. What happens as a result of this movement?

It is probable that the effect will at first be confined to the short-loan market. Bill rates and call-loan rates will be low. There will be a condition of ease and liquidity in the inner circle of financial institutions.

If such a state of affairs continues for long, however, it will begin to spread to the long-term market. It will be profitable to borrow from the banks to hold long-dated securities. There will be an upward movement in the market for bonds and debentures. There is no need to suppose that all this is financed by new credit. As the upward movement proceeds, people who have had money lying idle in the banks will be drawn into the movement. The existing supply of money will commence to circulate more rapidly.

It is not possible for a movement of this sort to proceed very far before it begins to affect other branches of the market. The fall in the yield of bonds and debentures, which is the obverse of the rise in their value, will lead the more adventurous spirits in the market to begin to look elsewhere for a higher return on their investment. The market in common stocks will rise. It will not be long before a stock exchange boom is in progress. If it is a country where development is expected, there will be extensive speculation too in real estate.

But a boom of this sort is not a thing which can be confined in its effects to the money market. The idea that a boom on the Stock Exchange keeps money from industry is of course the exact reverse of the truth. The rise in security prices makes it easier for existing undertakings to secure overdrafts from the banks. At the same time it is a direct incentive to the flotation of new issues. If the centre is financially important, part of this will probably take the form of foreign lending.

All this will be reflected in the various commodity markets. As the money raised in these different ways is spent, it will tend to drive up (or to prevent from falling) the prices of raw materials. The heavy industries will begin to make larger profits. This in turn will react on the market for securities. Prices will be marked up to reflect the higher expectations of profit. More money will be borrowed from the banks to finance speculative operations. The rapidity with which deposits are used will increase still further. The yield of gilt-edged securities will begin to rise. The opportunity for speculative gain will be such that short-loan rates will be driven above long. By this time the banks will have become alarmed and will be making various attempts to put the brake on. For some time, however, the wave of optimism may carry the boom along.

But it cannot go on. As it proceeds, the technical strain on the credit structure becomes greater and greater. At the same time, the rise in wage rates, re-inforced probably by the expenditure of speculative gains for consumptive purposes, diminishes the prospects of profitability of the industries producing capital-goods, both by raising their costs and by stimulating the competition of the consumption-good industries, thus raising the rate at which they can borrow. Usually it is some accident which is actually responsible for a reversal of the process—a conspicuous business failure, the rumour of a bad crop, or something fortuitous of that kind. But the end is certain. Once costs have begun to rise it would require a continuous increase in the rate of increase of credit to prevent the thing coming to disaster. But that itself, as we have seen in the great post-war inflations, would eventually generate panic. Sooner or later the initial errors are discovered. And then starts a reverse rush for liquidity. The Stock Exchange collapses. There is a stoppage of new issues. Production in the industries producing capital-goods slows down. The boom is at an end.

6. Finally, one more word about the origin of such movements. So far, for the sake of expository convenience, we have assumed that the expansion of credit was directly initiated by the banks. This is not unlikely. Indeed, as we shall see, there is strong reason to suppose that such was the origin of at least one important phase of the fluctuation we are discussing. But it is not at all necessary. The downward movement of the discount rate may be the result of the flow of new gold from the mines. It is equally possible that the expansion may originate on the "goods side". The conditions for credit expansion of the sort we have been discussing are present when, the structure of money rates remaining constant, there occurs some change in the sphere of production, some invention, some opening up of new markets, some discovery of new natural resources, which makes borrowing more profitable—to use a technical term, some change which tends to raise the "natural rate" of interest. If in such circumstances money rates are not raised, then there are present the conditions for an extension of borrowing, an introduction into circulation of new money, which brings it about that investment is in excess of saving.

Recognition of this point should do much to remove the misgivings which are often entertained with regard to "purely monetary" theories of the trade cycle. A purely monetary theory of the trade cycle—a theory which explained the ups and downs of trade solely in terms of movements of the general level of prices brought about by the arbitrary changes in monetary conditions—is quite rightly regarded with suspicion by most people who have had some experience of the working of the economic machine. If it were all as easy as that the trade cycle would have been eliminated already. If a mistake were made in one direction, it would be enough to reverse it by the converse monetary measures. The world we live in is not of this degree of simplicity.

But the theory we have been developing does not make this assumption. It allows for the impulse to expansion to come either from the condition of real investment or from changes in monetary policy. It exhibits at every point the changes in the world of productive activity which follow these initial impulses, and it shows them proceeding *via* changes in anticipation of the future of business men and investors. It explains the real over-production in certain lines of industry which arises as a result of these changes. It shows how, when the boom has collapsed, there exist dislocations and disproportionalities in the world of industry, the wreckage of false expectations, which monetary manipulation is not likely to remove. Only in its emphasis on the importance of demand in terms of money and the influence of money rates of interest as transmitted through investment markets can it be described as a monetary theory of the trade cycle. But in this form surely emphasis on monetary factors is only in accordance with common knowledge of the facts of business.

7. So far we have simply discovered how a general fluctuation of trade is logically possible. We have seen

how an inflation which operates through the mechanism of the money market may breed errors of anticipation among the capital-producing industries which lead first to the phenomena of a boom and then, when these errors are revealed, to a consequential collapse. How does this theory fit the facts of the present depression?

At this point it is necessary to proceed with great caution. Whatever be the ultimate truth with regard to the origin of this depression, one thing is certain, that no one explanation is capable of explaining all its different aspects. As we shall see in more detail in the next chapter, the fundamental causes, whatever they may be, have operated in a *milieu* more than usually disturbed by external changes and secondary oscillations, and their manifestations are thus inevitably complicated. It will take years of careful scrutiny of the available material before we can hope to be in a position to pronounce with complete confidence on these matters, and it is not certain that we shall ever reach this stage. Nevertheless, even now, there is a considerable body of evidence which seems to afford a presumption that causes, not dissimilar from the causes outlined above, have actually been in operation.

The big collapse came in America, and it is to America, and the centres most intimately associated with America, that we must turn if we are to discover the antecedents of the depression.

If we look in this direction we do certainly find movements remarkably similar to the movements we should expect from our theory. We saw in the last chapter what a very considerable expansion of credit took place in the Federal Reserve System from 1925 onwards. The following chart, which exhibits bank debits divided by bank deposits, gives a rough indication of the changes in the velocity of circulation during the same period:[1]

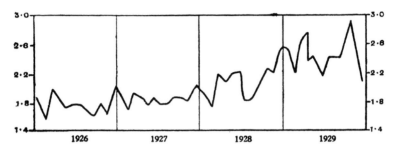

UNITED STATES—VELOCITY OF CIRCULATION OF BANK DEPOSITS

No doubt some of this was restricted to a very narrow field of speculative operations—though it should be observed that the index for the banks outside New York moves in the same direction as the New York index itself. But even when this has been fully discounted, it is evident, if we take both the increase in credit and the increase in velocity into account, that the increase in the effective volume of money was very great indeed—that there was undoubtedly a most considerable inflationary movement.

The effects of this are quite evident in the market for common stocks. The following chart shows the movement of the prices of such securities during the period under consideration.[2]

It is not necessary to labour the point that this was one of the most remarkable Stock Exchange booms in modern economic history.

Expectations are not disappointed when we turn

[1] For the figures on which it is based see Statistical Appendix, Table 15.
[2] For the figures see Statistical Appendix, Table 2.

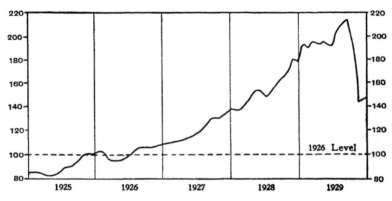

UNITED STATES—INDEX OF SECURITY PRICES

to the sphere of production. The following chart[1] shows the movement of the production of producers' goods and consumers' goods at this time. The indices from which it is constructed are not by any means all that could be desired from the point of view of statistical purity, but the general direction of movement is unmistakeable.

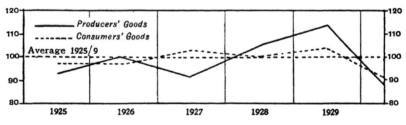

UNITED STATES—INDICES OF PRODUCTION

The construction of durable consumers' goods too shows a similar movement. The index of the value of residential building contracts awarded rises from 117 in 1927 to 126 in 1928. It then falls off as money rates become higher. In general we find all the characteristic evidences of a boom in the constructional and raw material producing industries.

[1] For the figures see Statistical Appendix, Table 9.

Similarly, when we turn to interest rates and costs
we find movements which conform to the expectations
of theory. The following chart shows movements of
short-loan rates of interest in New York City: [1]

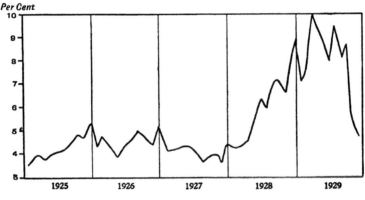

NEW YORK—CALL-LOAN RATE

Statistics of costs are hard to obtain. The wage index,
however, which stood at 212 in January 1925 and 221
in January 1927, had risen to 227 in September 1929.
Here we have just those directions of movement which
have been explained.

It is sometimes said that the movement of wage
rates is too small to have played the part here ascribed
to them. This objection is reinforced by appeal to the
comparatively small increase in the figures of national
income recorded during this period ($79 billions to
$85 billions). This seems to have little weight. This for
two reasons. In so far as the wage index is an index of
costs, it probably considerably under-estimates the
movement. All the evidence on trade fluctuation seems
to show that, during the later phases of a cycle, costs
rise faster than the movement of wage rates would
suggest. On the other hand, in so far as it is an index

[1] For the figures see Statistical Appendix, Table 21.

of increased pressure at the consumption end, it must be remembered that it again clearly errs on the side of under-estimation. During the later stages of the boom there seems reason to suppose that among many classes of consumers speculative gains were treated as income and spent accordingly. Moreover, statistics of national income are misleading here, since they include agricultural incomes which were actually falling during the period under consideration. So far as manufacturing industry is concerned there seems no reason to doubt that, towards the end of the boom, there occurred an increase in costs and a considerable increase of spending for consumptive purposes.

The one element which at first sight appears to be incompatible with the explanation we have offered is the movement of prices. In June 1924 the level of wholesale prices in the United States stood at 95.[1] In June 1927 it stood at 94. In June 1929 it stood at 95. The price-level was almost stationary—if anything, tending to fall slightly. At first sight this appears to be incompatible with the suggestion of an inflationary boom, and there can be no doubt that it was the more or less stable condition of the price-level which blinded contemporary observers to the real nature of what was going on at the time. So long as the price-level remains stationary, they urged, there can be no fear of inflation. A little reflection, however, should show that this belief is fallacious. A stationary price-level shows an absence of inflation only when production is stationary. When productivity is increasing, then, in the absence of inflation, we should expect prices to fall. Now the period we are examining was a period of rapidly increasing productivity. The

[1] For the figures see Statistical Appendix, Table 6.

comparative stability of prices, therefore, so far from being a proof of the absence of inflation, is a proof of its presence.

On this point the verdict of Mr. J. M. Keynes is particularly interesting. Mr. Keynes, it will be remembered, was not one of those who expressed alarm at the abundance of cheap money during the days of the expansion. On the contrary, he was one of the chief influences in the world calling for more and more cheap money. In the *Treatise on Money*, however, with customary candour, he admits having misapprehended the situation:

> Anyone who looked only at the index of prices would see no reason to suspect any material degree of inflation, whilst anyone who looked only at the total volume of bank credit and the prices of common stocks would have been convinced of the presence of an inflation actual or impending. For my part I took the view at the time that there was no inflation in the sense in which I use this term. Looking back in the light of fuller statistical information than was then available, I believe that whilst there was probably no material inflation up to the end of 1927, a genuine profit inflation developed some time between that date and the summer of 1929.[1]

On the existence of inflation in America during these years, therefore, there would appear to be substantial agreement. Would that this had been so then.

8. The inflation was not confined to America, although it was in that part of the world that some of its most characteristic manifestations were witnessed. An enormous volume of foreign loans spread out to other centres and generated expansion there. The following chart shows the movement of capital into Germany and the resulting credit expansion:[2]

---

[1] *A Treatise on Money*, vol. ii. p. 190.
[2] For the figures see Statistical Appendix, Tables 23, 24 and 25.

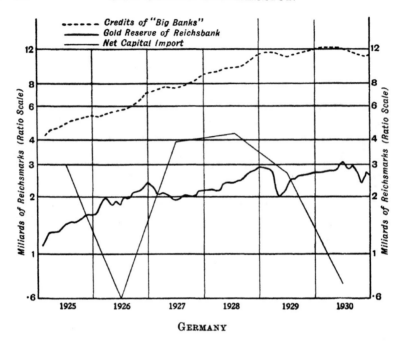

GERMANY

Security prices had reached a peak in the early part of 1927 from which they were shaken by efforts on the part of the Reichsbank to control the situation. But the inflowing tide of credit from the United States overbore this tendency to recession. In the later part of the year they revived and remained active until the end of 1928, when the inflow of foreign lending began to slacken. The discount rate which was 5 per cent in the early part of 1927 reached 7½ per cent in the spring of 1929. Wages rose. The index of skilled wages, for instance, which was 96 in the first quarter of 1927, by October 1929 had reached a level of 104. Other series show a similar movement. Here surely are characteristic symptoms of the effects of credit expansion.[1]

But the expansion did not stop here. It was almost world-wide in extent. It is difficult to compile an index

[1] For further figures see Statistical Appendix, Tables 26, 27 and 28.

of world expansion. The following table, based on statistics furnished by the League of Nations, gives some idea of the extent to which even not predominantly industrial countries were affected:

LOANS, DISCOUNTS AND ADVANCES OF COMMERCIAL BANKS

Country	1924	1929
Canada	100	162
Argentine	100	134
Brazil	100	151 (1928)
Australia	100	146
New Zealand . . .	100	122
Union of South Africa . .	100	181

These figures probably a little exaggerate the expansion for they are "corrected" for changes in the price-level, which fell slightly during the period. But it is difficult to understand the frame of mind of those who deny the existence of a very considerable degree of inflation.

9. But why did inflation take place?

It is clear that the effects of the war and the post-war inflation, which caused so large a proportion of the world's gold supply to be concentrated in New York, laid the foundations for the expansion. It has sometimes been said that these gold imports were sterilised. But, as we have seen, this is a complete misapprehension. They were made the basis of a very considerable expansion.

But clearly this is not the end of the story. If we look back at the chart of credit movements in the States which we were examining in the last chapter we shall see, as indeed we noticed then, that the system continued to expand in 1927–28, even when gold was flowing out. It is clear, too, from the velocity chart that it was during this period that the situation got really out of hand. Why did this take place?

The answer seems to be that it was the direct outcome of misdirected management on the part of the Federal Reserve authorities—an error of management, however, which Englishmen at any rate have no right to speak of with reproach, for it seems almost certain that it was carried out very largely with the intent to ease our position.

The situation seems to have been roughly as follows. By the spring of 1927 the upward movement of business in the United States, which started in 1925, showed signs of coming to a conclusion. A moderate depression was in sight. There is no reason to suppose that this depression would have been of very great duration or of unusual severity. It was a normal cyclical movement.

Meantime, however, events in England had produced a position of unusual difficulty and uncertainty. In 1925 the British authorities had restored the Gold Standard at a parity which, in the light of subsequent events, is now generally admitted to have been too high. The consequences were not long in appearing. Exports fell off. Imports increased. The Gold Standard was in peril. The effects of the over-valued exchange made themselves felt with greatest severity in the coal trade. Throughout 1926 there raged labour disputes, which were the direct consequence of these troubles— first the general strike, then a strike in the coal-fields which dragged out for over six months, still further endangering the trade balance. By 1927 the position was one of great danger. International assistance was sought. And in the summer of that year, partly in order to help us, partly in order to ease the domestic position, the authorities of the Federal Reserve System took the momentous step of forcing a régime of cheap money. A vigorous policy of purchasing securities was initiated.

On this point the evidence of Mr. A. C. Miller, the most experienced member of the Federal Reserve Board, before the Senate Committee on Banking and Currency, seems decisive:

> In the year 1927 . . . you will note the pronounced increase in these holdings [Federal Reserve holdings of United States securities] in the second half of the year. Coupled with the heavy purchases of acceptances it was the greatest and boldest operation ever undertaken by the Federal Reserve System, and, in my judgement, resulted in one of the most costly errors committed by it or any other banking system in the last 75 years! . . .[1]

> What was the object of Federal Reserve Policy in 1927? It was to bring down money rates, the call rate among them, because of the international importance the call rate had come to acquire. The purpose was to start an outflow of gold—to reverse the previous inflow of gold into this country.[2]

The policy succeeded. The impending recession was averted. The London position was eased. The reflation succeeded. Production and the Stock Exchange took on a new lease of life. But from that date, according to all the evidence, the situation got completely out of control. By 1928 the authorities were thoroughly frightened. But now the forces they had released were too strong for them. In vain they issued secret warnings. In vain they pushed up their own rates of dis-

---

[1] *Senate Hearings pursuant to S.R. 71*, 1931, p. 134.
[2] *Ibid.* p. 154.

count. Velocity of circulation, the frenzied anticipation of speculators and company promoters, had now taken control. With resignation the best men in the system looked forward to the inevitable smash.

Thus, in the last analysis, it was deliberate co-operation between Central bankers, deliberate "reflation" on the part of the Federal Reserve authorities, which produced the worst phase of this stupendous fluctuation. Far from showing the indifference to prevalent trends of opinion, of which they have so often been accused, it seems that they had learnt the lesson only too well. It was not old-fashioned practice but new-fashioned theory which was responsible for the excesses of the American disaster.

CHAPTER IV

THE CAUSES OF DEFLATION

1. A FLUCTUATION of the kind described in the last chapter is bound to be followed by a period of extensive depression. The errors of anticipation which led to the disaster have been discovered. Adjustment must be made to the new situation. While this takes place some factors of production will be unemployed, some funds of liquid capital will be left idle at the banks. Moreover, the general shock to confidence is likely to accentuate this process. Investors will fight shy of active investment. Bonds will be preferred to equities. More money will tend to be left on deposit. The coming of depression is almost certain to be accompanied by some measure of deflation.

But, in a system undisturbed by other causes making for depression, there seems no reason to suppose that this process need go very far. The experience of similar fluctuations in the pre-war period seems to suggest that, after a certain interval of liquidation and cost cutting, business prospects will once more brighten and revival will gradually take place. In the present depression things have been different. Whether or not revival is now on the way, there can be no doubt that the deflationary process which preceded it has been one of quite unparalleled severity. The explanation which we have examined already provides an account of how the slump originated. But it certainly does not explain why it has been so severe. Our next task, therefore, is to examine this problem. What have been the causes of the severity of the depression?

At the outset of the inquiry, one thing is clear. No single explanation of this phenomenon will be sufficient. The genesis of the slump may be traced to the collapse of a general inflationary movement which might be regarded as a single cause. But the subsequent course of the slump has been so obviously affected by a multiplicity of influences that any attempt to bring them under one heading must necessarily involve over-simplification. Political accidents, deliberate policies, structural weaknesses, local psychology, have all played a part which cannot be ignored. Nor is it possible at this stage to assign exact quantitative importance to these influences. Who can diagnose with certainty the relative importance of the part played by political power and the part played by bad banking policy, not to mention personal dishonesty, in the causation of the German Banking Crisis? What weight are we to assign to the peculiar psychology of the American people, what weight to the mechanical difficulties of their debt structure, in explaining the collapse of last spring? Clearly the time has not yet come, if it ever will, for exact assessment of exact causal priority in this history. All that can be done is to ascertain the existence of certain tendencies and to explain their mode of operation.

It will be convenient to examine, first, certain general characteristics of the political and economic structure in which the dislocation took place, and then subsequently to trace certain tendencies of policy which have aggravated the disturbance.

2. If we look at the general circumstances of the time in which the breakdown took place, it is not difficult to see that the probabilities of a depression more severe than most were very high.

It was a time of great political unrest. The Reparation problem was still unsettled. The political frontiers of Europe, then as always since the war, were the subject of hot dispute. Internally the various governments of the ex-enemy powers maintained an equilibrium ever more perilously poised half-way between democracy and dictatorship. The German position was especially acute. The tide of political extremism, which has since overwhelmed that country, was already rising strongly. The Nazi propaganda, hitherto confined to the worst elements of the ex-military and ex-criminal classes and to a handful of the less responsible students, was beginning to make itself felt in high politics. The German middle classes, bereft of their property during the inflation, their minds besodden with the turgid anti-rationalism which in that part of the world has for many decades passed as profundity, were apt soil for such teaching. Any worsening of the economic situation was likely to lead to political upheaval.

All this was itself conducive to a worsening of the economic situation. In a world of such uncertain political prospects, the prospects of enterprise were necessarily uncertain. The distribution of resources was distorted by the high political risk factor. As the situation deteriorated a vicious circle set in. The business depression reacted on politics and politics reacted on the business depression. Fears of the future set in motion forces which brought it about that these fears were justified. The view which ascribes the course of the depression to fluctuations of political confidence alone, no doubt involves considerable exaggeration. But a view which takes no account of politics omits one of the most important factors operative. The continual intensification of political risk is one of the dominant features of this period.

3. But politics apart, there were certain features of the general economic situation which were conducive to severity of depression. The profound dislocations brought about by the war, to which we have already alluded, had not yet been eliminated. The capital shortage in Germany and Central Europe involved a dislocation of the channels of investment unprecedented in modern economic history. Never have there existed between civilised areas such wide differences of rates of return on capital. While the boom lasted, foreign lending from American and from other centres to some extent submerged these differences. The industrial machine in Germany was attuned once more to relatively low rates of interest. But the moment foreign loans ceased to flow in this direction the capital shortage was once more revealed. The vast system of over-rationalised plant and equipment was paralysed for want of capital. In a normal fluctuation the probability is that the degree of error in long-term interest rates is not more than one or two per cent. In Germany and Central Europe it was probably two or three times this magnitude.

Beyond this, the technical changes of the post-war period, especially in agricultural production, had produced a situation in which the incidence of industrial depression was likely to be unusually severe. We have seen already that it is a fallacy to regard technical progress in any line of industry as being likely in itself to lead to general depression. But we have recognised also that if the result of technical progress in the shape of a great fall in the prices of the products concerned were to become manifest at a time at which other lines of industry were depressed, there might well be an enhancement of the general difficulties. This seems to have been what has happened. The fall of prices of agricultural products due to technical improvement has coincided with industrial depression, and the difficulties of transition have been heightened. This seems to be the core of truth in the popular views on this subject. It is important, however, not to press it too far. As we shall see, there is strong reason to believe that many of the difficulties created by the position in the markets for agricultural products are in fact by-products of State policy and the peculiar nature of the boom.

4. The effects of these changes were bound in any case to be extensive. But there can be little doubt that the difficulties with which they have been accompanied are, in part at any rate, a by-product of the weaknesses of the post-war economic structure. The effects of an earthquake are, in part, a function of the strength of the original shocks, in part a function of the strength of the buildings affected. So in the economic system the effects of fluctuations, whether cyclical or otherwise, are in part a function of the magnitude of the original change, in part a function of the elasticity of the economic organisation affected.

Now there can be no doubt that, in the post-war period, the capacity of the economic system to sustain shocks and to adapt itself to a process of rapid change has been seriously impaired. The essence of pre-war capitalism was the free market, not necessarily free competition in the remote and rigid sense of the mathematical economists; but the free market in the sense that the buying and selling of goods and the factors of production was not subject to arbitrary interference by the State or strong monopolistic controls. No doubt there was some interference and some monopoly. But that the free market was the typical institution is not open to serious question. Since the war it has tended to be more and more restricted. The cartelisation of industry, the growth of the strength of trade unions, the multiplication of State controls, have created an economic structure which, whatever its ethical or aesthetic superiority, is certainly much less capable of rapid adaptation to change than was the older more competitive system. This puts it very mildly. There can be little doubt, on a broad view, that the tendencies under discussion, so far from facilitating change or easing the process of transition, do indeed work in precisely the opposite direction. Certainly no one who wishes to understand the persistence of the maladjustments of the great slump can neglect the element of inelasticity and uncertainty introduced by the existence of the various pools and restriction schemes, the rigidities of the labour market and cartel prices, which are the characteristic manifestation of these developments.

These tendencies are the creation of policy. It is sometimes thought that they are the inevitable outcome of modern technical conditions. But this is not the case. Whether modern technical developments operating in a free system would give rise to such phenomena is a question which we may leave undiscussed. Historically, the fact is that the elements of rigidity and instability, which we are discussing, are the direct outcome of policy. So far in the history of the world cartels and labour organisations exercising strongly monopolistic influence have not shown themselves to be capable of survival, save as a result of direct or indirect assistance from States. We have seen already how the war-time controls fostered the growth of such bodies. The cartel systems of continental Europe are the direct creation of tariffs and State intervention. The post-war rigidity of wages is a by-product of Unemployment Insurance. So, too, with the great restriction schemes which have exerted such influence on the various commodity markets—Rubber Restriction, the Brazilian Coffee Institute, the Sugar Control, the Federal Farm Relief Agency, and so on. All are inconceivable without direct State intervention. Whether or not from what is called a "social" point of view these things have been justifiable, it is not open to serious question that their existence has introduced a new instability in the economic structure, and that this has had an important influence in the intensification of the slump.

5. To understand completely the peculiar dangers of the economic structure in which the slump began, it is necessary to turn once more to the circumstances of the boom which preceded it.

We have seen already that the genesis of the slump can be attributed to the effects of credit expansion. But, so far, our diagnosis has been confined to the quantitative aspects of this process—to its magnitude relatively to the movement of productivity and to its effects on industries with different investment periods. As a first approximation to the truth this procedure has justification. Any other mode of approach would involve missing the wood for the trees—missing the essential direction of change by preoccupation with details of particular movements Nevertheless, we do wrong to stop at this stage—to leave undiscussed the qualitative aspects of the credit expansion—for there can be no doubt that they are of high relevance to the explanation of the severity of the slump. The economist, listening to the business man as he attributes the whole disaster to this or that particularly monstrous piece of financial ineptitude or business chicanery, may well feel that these details alone put matters in a wrong perspective. But he pays the penalty of superficiality if he does not see that somewhere, somehow, they must form part of the total picture.

Now it is clear that an inflationary boom of the kind which was described in the last chapter, besides having the quantitative effect of over-stimulating the capital-goods industries, also has the qualitative effect of providing a favourable atmosphere for the fraudulent operations of sharks and swindlers. It is not when money is tight, when men look twice at each shilling before they spend it, that the Kreugers and Hatrys get away with it. It is when money is easy, when profits seem to be there for the taking and everyone is anxious to be in a little earlier than his neighbour. This has been the case in all the major booms of history. The big frauds almost all have been perpetrated on a rising market.

> Blest paper credit. Last and best supply
> To lend corruption lighter wings to fly,

sang Pope two hundred years ago. There is no need to multiply evidence of this influence of inflationary credit in the boom from whose aftermath we are still suffering.

But there is no doubt, too, that the latest frauds

were perpetrated upon a public which had become quite abnormally gullible. The scale of business, the air of *expertise* with which it was invested, the vast mechanism of the operations of high finance, were conducive to an attitude of mind in which the possibility of fraud or serious error was disregarded. No doubt before banks had big offices and expert advisers there was an "individualist chaos". But we had changed all that. As if the fact that a man had five telephones on his desk and a menagerie of tame statisticians in the cellar was a circumstance which justified the suspension of all the maxims of Victorian prudence! But they were suspended, and the mistakes which Victorian prudence had painfully learnt to avoid were committed.

But the boom was remarkable, not only for the proliferation of fashionable fraud; it was remarkable, too, for a change in the methods of straightforward financing. The history of post-war finance is marked by a conspicuous increase in the proportion of public investment which takes the form of fixed debt rather than participating ownership. This tendency was bound to accentuate the difficulties of any period of depression.

In part, the change was due to changes of banking policy. The increased participation by banks in the financing of all kinds of enterprise created a market for bonds where equities would have been unacceptable. The big insurance companies, moreover, through whose agency so large a proportion of the savings of the poorer and middle classes are invested, had a preference for this kind of investment.

But in part it was due to the increased economic activity of States and governmental bodies. The most intractable and disastrous masses of fixed debt which

have obstructed recovery in the slump have been
debts of this sort. The example of Australia will be
familiar to English investors. Even more conspicuous,
and much more important as an unsettling influence
in the depression, are the debts of the German and
Central European States and municipalities. Of the
total amount invested in Germany in the years 1924–
1928, it has been estimated that at least 40 per cent was
on account of governmental bodies. Much of this was
spent on the carrying out of works such as the construction of swimming-baths, the financing of housing
schemes and so on, which had little prospect of being
financially remunerative. This was at a time when
German industry was still suffering from the greatest
capital shortage in modern economic history. Much of
this money is irretrievably lost. But, because it was
borrowed by government bodies, recognition of this
fact is slow to come and liquidation has thus been
delayed. Paradoxically enough, economists who have
urged that this sort of thing has not proved its worth
in practice, are often called by their opponents
"deflationists".

Finally, in this connection, it should be noted that
the easy money conditions created by the boom had
an important influence in facilitating the rise of the
various pools and restriction schemes for agricultural
products to which allusion has been made already. It
is not to be thought that the Brazilian Coffee Institute,
for example, would have been able to raise the colossal
sums it did for so preposterous an adventure as the
"valorisation" of 1927–29 in a time in which men were
careful of the way they spent their money. Nor can it
be doubted that the general inflationary conditions
of that period served to support the prices of agricul-

tural products which in more normal circumstances would have been falling. To that extent, therefore, the process of readjustment was delayed, and the dislocation which was eventually revealed was made greater.

6. So far, we have done little but examine those various features of the general political and economic environment and the internal industrial structure of the pre-slump period which made it likely that the breakdown of the boom would be accompanied by more dislocations and disturbances than have usually accompanied the termination of prosperity in the past. We have now to examine certain tendencies of policy since that date which have greatly enhanced these difficulties.

We may commence with the policy of restrictions on international trade.

The use of protective tariffs as a "cure" for trade depression is not new. The atmosphere of trade depression is favourable to the adoption of panic measures. The interests which, in times of prosperity, find it hard to enlist support for their conspiracies to rob the public of the advantages of cheapness and division of labour, in times of bad trade, find a much more sympathetic hearing. People are alarmed. The dangers of a price-fall due to deflation blind them to the dangers of a price-rise due to restriction. The existence of unused capacity makes it easy for them to believe that no diminution of the volume of exports is likely to follow the imposition of restrictions on imports. As a consequence, whenever a depression occurs —that is, a general contraction of trade—there is to be witnessed the odd spectacle of the nations of the world zealously endeavouring to bring about a further contraction by excluding each other's products. In this way arose the protective systems of the latter part of the nineteenth century. In this respect the post-war world has not been slow to continue old practices.

But it has continued them on a scale which makes all previous trade restrictions insignificant by comparison. We have seen already the effects of this on the total value of world trade—contraction to something like a third of its former dimensions. An almost equally vivid illustration of what has happened is provided by the following table, which shows the domestic price of wheat in different countries in 1929 and 1932:[1]

Country	In United States Cents per Bushel of 60 lb.	
	January 1929	January 1932
Argentina	113	44
Canada	120	51
Great Britain	123	53
United States	121	58
India	158	60
Hungary	158	60
Poland	140	81
Sweden	137	91
Austria	131	120
Czechoslovakia . . .	147	121
Germany	135	147
Italy	192	151
France	164	179

From a state of affairs in which the price differences were at the most of the order of magnitude of 80 cents we have passed in three years to a state of affairs

[1] The figures are taken from the League of Nations *World Economic Survey, 1931-32*, p. 137.

in which they are 135 cents. In some centres the price of wheat has actually risen. In others it has fallen by almost 100 cents per bushel. To speak of a world price for wheat has now become an absurdity.

The effects of such obstructions are highly inimical to rapid recovery. That their long-run effects are to raise prices by restriction, and to limit the division of labour, need scarcely be argued. Only the feeble-minded and the paid agents of vested interests will be found to deny such propositions. But that their short-run effects are damaging to business improvement is not so immediately obvious. Yet in fact it is equally certain.

The short-run effect of the erection of obstructions to trade is a tendency to deflation. This is perhaps a hard saying for those who have come to look at tariffs as a means of safeguarding the trade balance and so avoiding deflation. But if we look at things from the international point of view, it is not so difficult to realise. It is clear that the effect of such obstructions is to destroy business capital. The effect of the curtailment of markets is to lower the value of stocks and of fixed capital devoted to making such stocks. This clearly tends to bring about forced sales and to increase the struggle for liquidity. At the same time, taking the world as a whole, it limits the field for the investment of new capital; that is to say, it lowers the equilibrium rate of interest. It follows, therefore, that unless money rates of interest immediately respond to this change in the conditions of real investment, the tendency for saving to lag behind investment, always present in the first stages of depression, will be enhanced.

There is a further effect also conducive to net

deflation. The erection of obstructions to trade has the effect of enhancing the difficulties of transferring debt payments from one centre to another. It should be noticed that the phrase used in this connection is the "erection of obstructions". It is not true, as is sometimes asserted, that the mere existence of tariffs makes transfer impossible. Nothing in theory or experience goes to suggest that this is correct. Given time, prices and costs in the different countries concerned can be adapted to carry through almost any degree of transfer over almost any degree of tariff obstacle. But if, as the price relationships which make this possible begin to emerge, new tariffs are erected to protect the creditor countries against the "devastating flood of cheap imports" which are the interest on their debts, then, of course, transfer is prevented and new adjustments have to take place. If the new tariffs come into operation as trade depression is developing, the probability is that the contraction of credit which they compel in the paying country will not be offset by any expansion in the receiving country. There will be a net deflation.

Now, of course, this is just what happened at the commencement of the present depression. When the flow of foreign lending from the United States began to cease it became necessary that the various debts owing to the United States and her citizens, which hitherto had been re-lent, should be paid in the form of goods. But just at the same time the Congress of the United States saw fit to put into force that monument of obstruction to trade, the Hawley-Smoot Tariff. There can be no doubt that the difficulties of the debtor countries were enormously enhanced by this. As has been shown in an earlier chapter, the accusation that the difficulties of the world had been enhanced by gold sterilisation on the part of the United States in the period 1923–29, has no foundation in fact. But that the introduction of the Hawley-Smoot Tariff at a critical stage of the depression did much damage is clear.

7. It would be a great mistake, however, to attribute the intensification of the crisis, particularly in its earlier stages, entirely to the influence of such obstacles. There were other policies adopted, the effect of which was no less serious.

The breakdown of an inflationary boom is a revelation of a wastage of capital. Large blocks of investment which have been made in the expectation of profit now prove to have no such prospect. It follows, therefore, that if profitability is to be restored costs must be cut and the capital resources rehabilitated.

In earlier depressions this has been the rule. And since the process has started quickly, comparatively little cutting has been necessary. But at the outset of this depression other measures were adopted. In the United States the word went forth that consumers' purchasing power must at all costs be maintained. President Hoover pledged the leaders of big industry to make no reduction of wage rates.[1] Until the summer of 1930 no serious reduction of wage rates took place. At the same time special efforts were made to maintain rates of dividends for shareholders. In Germany, too, throughout 1930 wage rates were well maintained.

Now this policy was the reverse of what was needed. As we have seen already, the depression is essentially a depression in the constructional and raw material

---

[1] See J. Viner, *Balanced Deflation, Inflation or More Depression,* University of Minnesota Press, 1933, pp. 12-13.

producing industries—a falling-off of demand for capital goods. As will be readily seen from the theory which has already been developed, one way of explaining the coming of depression is to say that demand at the consumers' end has become relatively too high. And, in fact, there was no deficiency of consumption at this period. Global statistics of consumption are almost impossible to obtain. But investigations made by the Harvard School of Business[1] indicate a state of affairs which is far from suggesting that consumers' buying was unduly slack. The following table exhibits some of the more spectacular results which the Harvard enquiry brings to light:

INDICES OF CONSUMPTION IN THE UNITED STATES

(1928 = 100)

Article	1928	1929	1930	1931	1932
Wheat flour .	100	100·2	101·0	94·5	90·0
Butter	100	101·5	101·8	104·4	105·6
Cheese	100	93·2	99·3	113·2	107·3
Gasolene	100	113·4	120·2	122·8	113·2
Cigarettes	100	112·4	112·9	107·1	97·8
Silks and velvets .	100	94·5	98·2	98·3	90·6
Hosiery	100	109·8	118·6	138·8	137·6
Infants' wear	100	107·5	106·8	105·4	91·4
Popular - priced dresses	100	113·5	115·3	125·5	117·7

These are admittedly strong cases. But it is clear that in many lines, consumption in 1930 was higher

[1] See Arthur R. Tebbutt, *The Behaviour of Consumption in Business Depression*, Harvard University Graduate School of Business Administration, August 1933. For the lower portion of the Table, which is based on physical sales of department stores, see p. 15. The other indices have been calculated.

than in the boom year 1929. In 1931 it was still high. Not until 1932 when the deflation which followed the financial crisis of 1931 had the system in its grip was there any important falling off. This is exactly what we should expect from the theory outlined in Chapter IV. But it is not a state of affairs which seems to call for the action which was taken.

In fact, the result of this action was to intensify the effects of the boom. The maintenance of wage rates and dividends was at the expense of capital. There can be little doubt that it was financed by encroachment on secret reserves. But what does this mean? Simply that the new saving of the community which takes up the sale of securities that constitute hidden reserves, instead of constituting new demand for the products of the capital-goods producing industries, is appropriated for the consumption of wage earners and dividend receivers. Consumption is maintained at the expense of capital. The powers of resistance of the capital-producing industries are sapped, and the struggle for liquidity is intensified. Thus, when cost cutting actually began, the cuts which were necessary if profitability was to be restored were very much greater and very much more disturbing to general confidence than would have been the case if the process had not been so long delayed.

8. The policy of maintaining consumers' purchasing power was of limited application and duration. Much more damaging and productive of general deflation have been the policies adopted in regard to debts and bad business positions in general. For these have been almost universally adopted.

In the course of a boom many bad business commitments are undertaken. Debts are incurred which it is impossible to repay. Stocks are produced and accumulated which it is impossible to sell at a profit. Loans are made which it is impossible to recover. Both in the sphere of finance and in the sphere of production, when the boom breaks, these bad commitments are revealed.

Now in order that revival may commence again, it is essential that these positions should be liquidated. There is nothing which is more damaging to confidence, nothing therefore which is more deflationary, than the persistence on a large scale of bad business positions. They affect the whole business atmosphere. The word goes round that such and such a house is in difficulties. People say, "It's only a matter of time before a crash comes. When it comes it may hit us too." Hence, even if their own position is perfectly sound, they begin to draw in their horns to make their position more liquid. So too in the commodity markets. If stocks are hanging over the market, even if for the time being prices have not fallen, people become nervous. They say, "The thing cannot last. It would be foolish to buy extensively." So hand-to-mouth buying sets in. The fear of a break is often much worse than the break itself.

Now in the pre-war busin ss depression a very clear policy had been developed to deal with this situation. The maxim adopted by central banks for dealing with financial crises was to discount freely on good security, but to keep the rate of discount high. Similarly in dealing with the wider dislocations of commodity prices and production no attempt was made to bring about artificially easy conditions. The results of this were simple. Firms whose position was fundamentally sound obtained what relief was necessary. Having confidence in the future, they were prepared to foot the bill. But the firms whose position was fundamentally unsound realised that the game was up and went into liquidation. After a short period of distress the stage was once more set for business recovery.

In the present depression we have changed all that. We eschew the sharp purge. We prefer the lingering disease. Everywhere, in the money market, in the commodity markets and in the broad field of company finance and public indebtedness, the efforts of Central Banks and Governments have been directed to propping up bad business positions.

We can see this most vividly in the sphere of Central Banking policy. The moment the boom broke in 1929, the Central Banks of the world, acting obviously in concert, set to work to create a condition of easy money, quite out of relation to the general conditions of the money market.[1] This policy was backed up by vigorous purchases of securities in the open market in the United States of America. From October 1929 to December 1930 no less than $410 millions was pumped into the market in this way. The result was as might have been expected. The process of liquidation was arrested. New loans were floated. The following table shows the issues on foreign account alone in the principal investment centres for the years 1928 to 1932:[2]

---

[1] See Statistical Appendix, Tables 28, 29, 30 and 31.

[2] This table, which relates to foreign issues in the United States, United Kingdom, Netherlands and Switzerland, is reproduced from Timoshenko, *World Agriculture and the Depression* (University of Michigan, 1933), p. 625. The original data are from the German *Institut für Konjunkturforschung*, with the exception of those for the fourth quarter of 1931, which have been taken from the article by F. Sternberg, "Die Weltwirtschaftskrisis," *Weltwirtschaftliches Archiv*, vol. 36, Heft 1 (July 1932), p. 131.

FOREIGN ISSUES ON FOUR SECURITY MARKETS

(In Millions of Dollars)

Period	1928	1929	1930	1931
First quarter . .	636·3	584·8	491·7	277·0
Second quarter .	754·9	373·5	727·3	169·6
Third quarter .	324·7	132·0	184·4	68·1
Fourth quarter .	386·4	194·9	304·0	0·5
Annual Total .	2102·3	1285·2	1707·4	515·2

It will be seen that the issues in the second quarter of 1930 were of an order of magnitude comparable with the issues of the corresponding quarter of 1928. This money was not soundly invested. For the most part it went to prop up positions which were fundamentally unsound. The easy conditions in the money market then and later on made possible the carrying of stocks which otherwise would have had to be sold off. The fundamental causes of uncertainty and deflation were not removed. It is clear from their magnitude that they could not be removed in this way. The reflation merely helped them to persist.

But this was not all. The policy of relief was not confined to the money markets. Everywhere the Governments of the world, fearing the effects of a break, intervened in one way or another to support weak positions. We have noted already the multiplication of tariffs. More direct forms of support were almost equally prevalent. The expenditure of the Federal Farm Board, the Reconstruction Finance Corporation, the renewed support to restriction schemes of one kind or another, are only the most conspicuous cases of a policy which was universal. The effects we know: continuation of uncertainty, intensification of the deflation, prolongation of the depression.

It is important to realise the nature of this diagnosis. It is not difficult for its critics, who are often people with something to save from the wreck themselves, to misrepresent it as a plea for bankruptcy as such. But this is not the case. Nobody wishes for bankruptcies. Nobody likes liquidation as such. If bankruptcy and liquidation can be avoided by sound financing nobody would be against such measures. All that is contended is that when the extent of mal-investment and over-indebtedness has passed a certain limit, measures which postpone liquidation only tend to make matters worse. No doubt in the first years of depression, to those who held short views of the disturbance, anything seemed preferable to a smash. But is it really clear, in the fourth year of depression, that a more astringent policy in 1930 would have been likely to cause more disturbance and dislocation than the dislocation and disturbance which have actually been caused by its postponement?

CHAPTER V

1. DEFLATION, when it springs from causes such as those discussed in the last chapter, is likely to have a cumulative influence. In the summer of 1931 the depression deepened into a great financial crisis, a crisis from whose disruptive effects the whole world is still suffering and is likely long to suffer. To understand this event and its consequences it is necessary to devote some attention to the peculiar economic circumstances of Great Britain. Great Britain is the storm-centre of this phase of the depression.

2. At the outbreak of the war, Great Britain, in common with all the other belligerent countries, abandoned the Gold Standard. At the end of 1919 the external value of the pound sterling in terms of gold dollars showed a depreciation of 22 per cent. Internal prices had more than doubled. Money-wages, if they had not kept pace with prices, at any rate had not lagged far behind.[1] For a short time the inflation continued. But it was not long before it was arrested. By 1921 the post-war boom was at an end.

As soon as this had happened there emerged an important issue of policy. What was to be the future basis of the British Monetary System? Was it to continue to be inconvertible paper without a gold backing

---

[1] See Tables 33 and 34, Statistical Appendix.

as it had been during the war? Or was it once more to be linked up to gold as it was before the war? And if so, at what rate of exchange was the return to gold to take place? These questions were the subject of long, and often heated, discussion.

In fact, however, there was only one question which had practical importance—the question of the correct gold parity. From the point of view of the historian of the recent crisis, nothing can be more important than the propaganda for a managed currency. It encouraged the belief that the stable price-level was the be-all and end-all of monetary policy. It created an attitude of mind on the part of the educated public which in subsequent years made it more and more difficult to work the Gold Standard successfully. It led to an extravagant admiration of the policy of the Federal Reserve System at a time when the policy of the Federal Reserve System was sowing the seeds of the slump. One of the main obstacles to the restoration of stable monetary conditions at the present day is the public opinion which this propaganda has engendered.

But from the point of view of immediate practice all this was a side-issue. At that time the idea of a managed currency never had a ghost of a chance of being adopted as a basis of policy. This for very good reasons. The state of the world at large was not such as to justify high hopes in the ability of Governments to manage inconvertible paper successfully. All the Great Powers, save America, had gone off the Gold Standard during the war. None of them had exhibited the capacity to keep the operation of the printing press within limits. At the time when the controversy in England was at its height, the standards of continental Europe were in a condition of the most violent fluctuation ever witnessed.

Trade had shrunk to a fraction of its pre-war dimensions. The one hope of stabilising business conditions seemed to be the elimination of these fluctuations. Gold stood for stability. The eyes of the world looked to Great Britain for leadership. Small wonder that responsible men charged with the conduct of policy, although ignorant for the most part of the profound theoretical strictures which could have been passed upon the plan for a managed currency, turned a deaf ear to all this talk and resolved upon a restoration of the Gold Standard.

But at what rate was it to be restored? Were we to go back to the old Gold Standard with the pound worth 123·27 grains of fine gold and the dollar-sterling exchange at 4·86? Or were we to devaluate to restore the Gold Standard at some lower parity? Here was a question of severely practical import. To go back to the old parity safely involved a rise of prices in America—the leading gold centre—a fall of prices at home, or some combination of these circumstances, which would bring prices and costs in Great Britain and the gold-using centres into the appropriate relationship. To devaluate at the parity of the moment meant none of these difficulties—meant the elimination of the waiting period, the avoidance of the stresses and strains of deflation. Yet curiously enough it was a policy which was hardly discussed. It was almost taken for granted that the Gold Standard should be restored at the old parity.

Why did this happen?

A combination of causes conspired to bring it about. Sentiment played a part. It was thought to be a fine thing for the pound once more to "look the dollar in the face". It was thought, too, that a return at the old rate would redound to the prestige of the City and so bring international business in greater volume to this country. There was some regard for the real value of sterling debts abroad, some regard for what was thought to be justice to the bond-holder. Partly it was due to a belief that American prices would rise and so obviate the need for deflation, partly to an ignorance of the difficulties which the degree of deflation otherwise necessary would involve. Beyond this we must not ignore the confusion created by the propaganda for a managed currency. In their eagerness to combat the views of the advocates of paper, the protagonists of the Gold Standard tended to assume that there was only one alternative to such a system—the Gold Standard at the old rate. In the clamour of this discussion, the few voices which urged devaluation tended to pass unheard.

It is not easy at this distance of time to do full justice to the undoubted sincerity and public spirit of those who held these opinions. There seems little in the argument for prestige. There could have been little loss of prestige in recognising changed conditions. Nor is there much in the argument for justice to the bond-holder. The object of policy was to restore the dollar-sterling exchange to the old parity. This could come about by a deflation of English prices, an inflation of American prices or an inflation of English prices accompanied by a still greater inflation in America, etc. etc.—"justice to the bond-holder", therefore, was a highly ambiguous notion. No doubt there was more in the argument for retaining the full value of sterling debts from abroad. But it is doubtful whether the sacrifices here would have outweighed the advantages of stabilisation in 1921 without the difficulties of deflation. As for the traditional wisdom of the subject, had not Ricardo a hundred years before made it perfectly clear that, whereas to redress a 5 per cent depreciation it was worth making a special effort, to redress a depreciation of 20 per cent was a game not worth the candle?

But restoration at the old parity was chosen. Throughout 1921 there was considerable deflation. Prices fell from 325 in April 1920 to 164 in January 1922. The dollar-sterling exchange rose to 4·221. From 1922 there ensued a period of uncertainty and indecision. The British price-index remained relatively stable; it was 160 in March 1922 and 165 in the same month of 1924. American prices rose from 95 in the second quarter of 1922 to 102 in the second quarter of 1923. They then relapsed to 96 in the second quarter of 1924. The exchange moved accordingly—4·44 in the second quarter of 1922, 4·63 in the second quarter of 1923, 4·34 in the second quarter of 1924. By the middle of 1924, however, matters took a decisive turn. American prices began to rise. By the first quarter of 1925 they had risen 8 per cent (from 96 to 104) while British prices only rose from 164 to 169 (quarterly averages)—roughly 4 per cent. In the foreign exchange markets a return to gold at the old parity was anticipated. The sterling-dollar exchange appreciated from 4·34 to 4·78.

In the spring of 1925, therefore, it was thought that the adjustment between sterling and gold prices was sufficiently close to warrant a resumption of gold payments at the old parity. Accordingly, on April 28th, 1925, gold payments were resumed. Great Britain had returned to the Gold Standard.

3. From 1925 onwards British industry was in diffi-

culties. Unemployment persisted at a high figure. In October 1924 it was 1,281,000. In the same month of 1929 it was 1,254,000. The export industries were stagnant and in some instances declining. Large expanses of the industrial North were more severely depressed than at any time since their rise. It is important not to exaggerate the dark side of the picture. Some industries in the South were going ahead fairly rapidly. Others were at least holding their own. The real wages of those in employment rose rapidly. But in a world in which, in most parts, trade appeared to be very prosperous, the mediocrity of our circumstances was conspicuous.

Why was this? Was it the result of a return to the Gold Standard at too high a parity? Or were other causes operative?

Even to-day it is not easy to give a precise answer to this question. Broadly speaking, the various explanations which have been put forward do not seem mutually exclusive. Controversial discussion of the question of the parity has made it quite clear that too much weight should not be attached to precise estimates of the degree to which sterling was over-valued when the return to gold took place. But that there was some over-valuation seems unquestionable. Admission of this, however, does not preclude appeal to other factors, the falling off of markets in the East, competition in the European markets for coal, the rise of manufacturing industry in other countries and so on, which tended further to aggravate the position. Indeed, an eclectic view seems most reasonable. The parity was too high. Our position in world markets declined also for other reasons.

But, whatever the rights and wrongs of this most

intricate question, one thing is certain. We were out of equilibrium. And the steps necessary to restore equilibrium were not taken.

It is quite clear that there was disequilibrium in the labour market. During the period under discussion the total number of unemployed never fell seriously below the level of a million. It was often considerably higher. Now the labour market is like all other markets in that the quantity sold—the amount of labour employed—is a function of price. If the price which prevails is above a certain point, then the market is not cleared—there is labour unemployed. Of course in times of the briskest trade and the freest labour market there will be some unemployment due to the process of industrial change, just as, during the best times in the real estate market, there will be houses vacant due to the turnover of population. But the unemployment of the period 1925–29 considerably exceeded the most generous estimate of the necessary minimum of this kind. The very fact, therefore, that there was unemployment on this scale is a proof that, in some parts of the labour market, the rates charged were too high.

This is not to say, as might wrongly be inferred, that the total amount paid as wages was too high. That does not follow at all. There are strong reasons for believing that the demand for labour of the less specialised kind has a considerable degree of elasticity. If that is so, then a reduction of wage rates would have been accompanied by an actual increase in the amount paid as wages. The main import of the diagnosis is missed if this distinction is not observed.

Nor is it to argue that unemployment was due to a policy of aggressive rate-raising. This may be the case in certain instances. It is fairly clear that it was so in Germany during this period. There are other cases equally conspicuous. But in Great Britain this was not so. Wage rates in Great Britain were more or less constant from 1924 onwards. All that happened was that, in the face of a tendency to a decline in the demand for labour, wage rates were not lowered. The causes of the change in the conditions of the market did not originate with the trade unions. If the analysis given above is correct, they originated partly in monetary policy and partly in changes in world markets. But the effects on the volume of unemployment were the same as would have been the case if they had. If the equilibrium price falls and the actual price remains unaltered, the market is not cleared.

But why was such a disequilibrium possible? In the pre-war period the persistence of unemployment at such a level was unheard of. The trade union percentage of unemployed in Great Britain only exceeded the lowest point of post-war unemployment twice during the fifty years for which we have records. The cause is evident. In the pre-war period the trade unions were responsible for the maintenance of their unemployed. If the volume of unemployment rose above a certain point they knew that it was time to reconsider their wage policy. (We owe our excellent unemployment statistics to the care with which they watched such movements.) In the post-war period they have been relieved of this responsibility by the system of unemployment insurance. The volume of unemployment created by their wage policy is therefore no longer a first consideration with their leaders. This is no indictment of the trade union leaders. Nor is it, in itself, a criticism of the system of unemployment insurance. It is simply a statement of unescapable fact. It is one of the consequences of unemployment insurance in the form in which it existed during that period that it increased the rigidity of wages. In a period when the equilibrium wage tends to fall this means disequilibrium in the labour market.

But this was not the only disequilibrium of that period. It is no less clear that the money market was in disequilibrium. We have examined the nature of this disequilibrium in Chapter II., when discussing the distribution of gold. All through the period from 1925 to 1929 the condition of the money market was abnormal. The dollar-sterling exchange tended continually towards the gold export point, as may be seen from the following figure:[1]

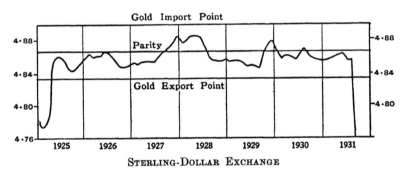

STERLING-DOLLAR EXCHANGE

The net increase in the reserve from April 1925 to April 1929 was about £3 millions. During the same period the world's monetary resources increased from about £10,244 millions to about £11,201 millions.

In such circumstances, as was only natural, there was continual anxiety about foreign lending. The market, which in pre-war days had cheerfully carried

[1] For the figures on which it is based see Statistical Appendix, Table 32.

an annual volume of anything up to £190 millions, now felt alarmed at movements less than half this size although in the meantime the value of money had fallen by 40 per cent. On at least two occasions, an embargo was placed on foreign issues by the Bank of England; and rumour speaks of less public restraints whose operation was almost continuous.

Such a state of affairs is clearly indicative of acute disequilibrium—a condition for which, failing a miracle elsewhere, the only remedy was a contraction of credit—a contraction of credit which would bring prices and costs into such a relation with the outside world that the tendency to lose gold would be arrested and the condition of stringency eased. But no such contraction took place. Micawber-like, the authorities sat waiting for something to turn up which would avoid the necessity for this disagreeable operation, meanwhile, on occasion, taking such steps as would prevent the loss of gold from having any effect on the market. "You will find, if you look at a succession of Bank Returns," said Sir Ernest Harvey, Deputy Governor of the Bank of England, in his evidence before the Macmillan Committee, referring to an occasion of this sort, "that the amount of gold we have lost has been almost replaced by an increase in the Bank's securities." Such a policy was bound to perpetuate the trouble. If, as gold flows out, credit is not contracted, then the occasion for the gold flow is not removed. The monetary reformers who, during these years, complained so bitterly that the Bank was deaf to their teaching, complained too much. Unostentatiously, without any public repudiation of Gold Standard practice, the Bank was following their policy.

It is clear that in such conditions the persistence of disequilibrium was almost inevitable. The initial occasion of disequilibrium, the precise weights to be assigned to the over-valuation of 1925, and to the adverse market conditions subsequently operative, may still be the subject of dispute. But the persistence of disequilibrium, however occasioned, is only to be explained as a failure of the internal mechanism to adapt itself to changed conditions—a failure which was due to the factors we have examined, a wage-level which was rigid and a credit mechanism which did not contract. Great Britain was not the only country to stabilise her exchange at the pre-war level. But, as Mr. Loveday has shown in an essay whose main findings are not open to serious question, she was the only country to fail to recover from such a policy. The following table, taken from this essay, shows the percentage movement of the gold value of exports of those European countries which re-established the pre-war level of their currencies:[1]

GOLD VALUE OF EXPORTS—PERCENTAGE MOVEMENT

Country	1913	1924	1925	1926	1927	1928	1929
United Kingdom .	100	138·4	146	*124*	135	137	136·6
Denmark . .	100	194	221	216	*226*	241	251
Norway . .	100	142	184	174	173	*176*	194
Sweden . .	100	*153*	167	174	198	193	221
Switzerland . .	100	146	*148*	133	146	154	151
Netherlands . .	..	100	*114*	110	120	126	126

(The figure for the first year during the whole of which the exchanges were at par is printed in italics.)

[1] See Loveday, *Britain and World Trade*, London, 1931, p. 158.

It will be seen that of the countries concerned only the United Kingdom failed to recover a level of exports at least as high as that prevailing before the restoration of the old parity. As Mr. Loveday concludes, the restoration of the old parity was more detrimental in England than elsewhere, "because other countries made the necessary adjustments to their whole machinery of production and we did not".

4. There was no boom in Great Britain. There were repercussions of the boom which was taking place elsewhere but no direct inflationary disturbance.[1] In consequence, the direct impact of depression was lighter. The slump, when it came, revealed no such gross internal mal-investments as were generally revealed elsewhere. The effects of the slump showed themselves in the first instance far more in a falling-off of demand from countries where the boom had been rampant than in any grave internal maladjustment. This showed itself in the statistics. The Board of Trade Index of Production for the third quarter of 1930, for instance, shows a decline of 10 per cent. In Germany over the same period there was a decline of 20 per cent; in the United States of America a decline of 23 per cent. The increase of unemployment between September 1929 and September 1930 shows a similar tendency. In Great Britain it increased 82 per cent and in Germany 116 per cent. Although no accurate information is available regarding unemployment in the United States, there is a consilience of evidence that the position of Great Britain in the

---

[1] It should be noted that this is not in the least in conflict with the view expressed in the last section that the price structure was in an inflated condition compared with the equilibrium level; nor with the view expressed in an earlier chapter that British disequilibrium was indirectly responsible for some of the inflation elsewhere.

slump, in respect of production, was perceptibly less bad than that of many other countries.

None the less, viewed as a whole, it was a position of great danger. We have seen already how insecure was the general position of London as a centre of world finance during the preceding period of prosperity. In the slump this insecurity was enhanced by the operation of a new factor. Hitherto there had been a certain reserve margin of safety in the magnitude of the volume of interest on investments overseas. So long as this continued to mount from year to year, the diminution of overseas lending which could be brought about by a rise in the discount rate could be trusted to restore for the moment the conditions of safety for the Gold Standard. This reserve was now to be depleted. The coming of depression in the lands in which British capital had been invested led to a falling-off of dividends. As it deepened, there was a decline in other more dependable receipts due to the suspension of debenture interest and default on governmental obligations. In 1929 the estimated net income from overseas investment was £250,000,000; in 1930 it was £220,000,000; in 1931, £165,000,000. In the same period, exports fell from £729,000,000 to £389,000,000 and shipping earnings from £65,000,000 to £30,000,000.[1] Clearly, unless steps were taken to remedy the local disequilibrium, the maintenance of the Gold Standard by Great Britain was likely to be a matter of increasing difficulty.

5. The difficulty thus created would have been great enough in the case of a subsidiary monetary system. It was increased beyond all comparison by the special circumstances of London as a world financial centre—

[1] See Table 35, Statistical Appendix.

by the presence of unusually large volumes of foreign balances liable to be withdrawn at very short notice.

The presence of these balances is to be attributed to a variety of causes. Monetary stabilisation in continental Europe had, in many cases, resulted in the establishment, not of independent Gold Standards of the British pre-war type, but of what were known as Gold Exchange Standards—currency systems in which the reserve of the Central Bank concerned consisted not of gold itself but of titles to gold held in another centre, such as London or New York, where gold was freely obtainable. The saving in expense of such arrangements was obvious, for the reserves so held were remunerative. But they tended to the erection of a credit structure larger than would otherwise have been possible and they concentrated the risk of withdrawal on the few main centres on which they depended. London was the chief of these centres, and in the period after 1925 a large volume of balances was continually held in London on foreign Central Bank account.

Such balances were a normal feature of the post-war monetary system. Had that system persisted they would necessarily have persisted with it. There were other balances, however, whose presence was not so normal. In the period from 1924 to 1926, when the French franc was depreciating and its future was highly uncertain, large volumes of French funds were placed for safety in this country. When the franc was stabilised these funds were not immediately repatriated. The French banks, into whose hands these assets gradually drifted, retained them in London to take advantage of the higher rates of interest there prevailing. It is said that, in times of difficulty, appeals were made that they should not be withdrawn too quickly. These appeals were not unsuccessful. In this way there remained right up to the crisis of 1931 an unusually large volume of French money on short loan in the City.

Beyond this, there was a miscellaneous volume of international money whose presence was to be explained partly in terms of straightforward commercial and financial convenience, partly, however, in terms of the peculiar circumstances of the post-war capital market. There seems little doubt that, since the war, there have existed very abnormal conditions in the European capital market. The supply of short-term funds relatively to the supply of money for long-term investment has been much greater than in the pre-war period—a condition which has been reflected in the relation between short- and long-term rates of interest. This has been due to many factors. Partly it is to be explained in terms of political risks which have scared the investor from certain forms of long-term investment; partly in terms of the provision by Governments, especially by the British Government, of short-term securities and bills which were thought to provide immunity from the risks of other forms of investment. Nor must we overlook, in this connection, the fundamental fact of the British international trade disequilibrium, whereby the chief European centre for long-term lending was chronically prevented from discharging its function of providing for the world at large an ample stream of foreign securities for long-term investment. But whatever the cause, in particular instances, the net effect was the same—an abnormally large fund of international short money flitting from one centre to another according to the variations in local conditions of risk and opportunities of profit. In the days before the crisis London was the habitation of a large proportion of this fund.

Now the presence of all these balances was not in itself a bad thing for the City. To judge from the language which was sometimes used when the abandonment of the Gold Standard had deprived such balances as remained of 25 per cent of their value, one would think that they had been accommodated here solely for charitable reasons. That was certainly not the case. They were a source of very considerable profit. But at the same time they were a source of considerable danger. If, at any time, confidence in London was shaken, a sudden withdrawal would lead to a very grave crisis.

6. The crisis came. Throughout the years since the war, the inhabitants of the Republic of Austria had been gradually consuming their capital. The trade policies of the secession States had limited the Austrian markets. The economic policy of successive Austrian governments and the Viennese municipality accelerated the process which the Paris Settlement had begun. From 1913 to 1930 the value of the Austrian industrial share capital situated in the present Austria shrank to a fifth of its former dimensions.[1] The expenditure of the Viennese municipality on its housing programme alone since the Armistice exceeded the total value of the capital of all Austrian manufacturing joint-stock companies.[2] In the year 1931 it was calculated that if all the undertakings in Austria were to be sold at the value of their Stock Exchange quotation for the

---

[1] The figures are given in an article by Dr. Oskar Morgenstern in the *Zeitschrift für Nationalökonomie*, Bd. iii. pp. 251-5.

[2] See Hayek, "Wirkungen des Mietzinsbeschränkungen," *Schriften des Vereins für Sozialpolitik*, Bd. 182, p. 265.

autumn of that year, the proceeds would not cover one-half of the public expenditure for a single year.

No financial system could stand such a strain as this without collapse. One by one, the financial houses in Vienna put up their shutters. The slump intensified the capital consumption. Early in May 1931, the Kredit Anstalt, which had taken over the bad debts of its predecessors, announced that it could not meet its liabilities. The actual smash is sometimes attributed to the political tension aroused by the untimely proposals for an economic *Anschluss* between Germany and Austria. Whether this is so or not, there can be no doubt that the ultimate cause of the difficulty was the capital consumption of the years which had preceded it.[1]

The collapse was the beginning of a world-wide financial crisis. The process of deflation analysed in an earlier chapter, together with the growing political tension which accompanied the rise of Hitler, had produced a situation of extreme peril in Germany in particular. The German banks, weakened by practices which for years had been the admiration of foreign financial experts—active participation in industrial financing—and honeycombed with the jobbery and graft characteristic of the Kreuger period, were in no position to stand a run. A run developed. American and French creditors hastened to withdraw their balances from Berlin. Domestic withdrawals began on

[1] On the whole Austrian episode, to which much too little attention has been given in English-speaking countries, the important paper by Mr. Nicholas Kaldor on "The Economic Situation of Austria", *Harvard Business Review*, October 1932, should be consulted. Austria is the classical example of how the various policies now being vigorously introduced into this and other countries actually work out in practice. The contention that it is *all* the result of the Peace Treaties does not bear examination. The Peace Treaties did much. But much, too, is the result of policy.

a large scale. Feverish attempts were made on all sides to arrest the rot. The Hoover moratorium was the most conspicuous. But in vain. On the morning of July 13th, the Danat Bank closed its doors, never to be reopened. The next day all banks in Berlin, save the Reichsbank, were closed by decree.

The crisis in Berlin was bound to have serious repercussions in London. The London bankers, drawing upon the ample supplies of international short money at their disposal, had made liberal advances to German banks and industry. When the run developed they had been slow to follow their American and French colleagues in withdrawing their advances. When the smash came and the Berlin banks were closed, therefore, their German assets were frozen. Important houses were believed to be heavily committed. The foreign creditors of London became nervous for the safety of their sterling assets. There began a run on sterling.

How far these fears would have gone had confidence in London otherwise been general it is impossible to say. But there existed no such confidence. For years, Continental opinion had been coming to the view that the British system was dying of ossification. The inflexibility of the wage-level, the drain on the Government finances of the colossal expenditure on unemployment relief, the incessant propaganda for cheap money, were widely noted. Englishmen travelling on the Continent in those years speedily became aware that, from the European point of view, these were the conspicuous features of the economic position of Great Britain. Rightly or wrongly, the Continent had come to the conclusion that if serious strain were to occur the adjustments necessary to remain on the Gold

Standard would not be made. The rejection by all three parties of the recommendations of the interim report of the Royal Commission on Unemployment Insurance only confirmed this opinion. The publication of the May report served to communicate something of this alarm to Englishmen. The run on sterling was intensified. Apprehension became general.

In these circumstances the measures taken to meet the crisis were not such as to restore confidence. Indeed, so far as foreign opinion was concerned, they only served to weaken it. Large sums were borrowed from France and the United States in the attempt to stave off disaster. Now there was very good warrant in earlier financial history for the adoption of such a measure. It was not the first time that the Bank of England had had resort to foreign borrowing when faced with financial difficulties. The immense resources of the Bank of France traditionally constituted a reserve line of defence when London was in difficulty. But there was this difference: in earlier crises the borrowing had been accompanied by high rates of discount. On this occasion the rate never rose above $4\frac{1}{2}$ per cent. Moreover, there was made permissible an increase in the fiduciary circulation.

If we are to understand the Continental point of view the significance of these facts cannot be overstated. Ever since the war, British financial experts had been travelling round Europe saying to distressed Governments: "You must put up your bank rate and you must limit your fiduciary issue. Anything else is bad finance." And now when the British crisis arrived we were observed to do neither of these things. The bank rate was kept low and we raised the fiduciary limit. It is said that the circumstances were different, that the functioning of English institutions is exempt from the criteria which Englishmen frame for the judgment of other people's policy. But it is scarcely to be wondered at that other people do not understand this; and that the foreigner, still smarting from the lessons of domestic inflation, thought that what was sauce for the goose was sauce for the gander, and continued to withdraw his money.

It is sometimes urged that if the bank rate had been raised it would only have made matters worse. People would have said, "The crisis is really serious now", and would have withdrawn their money all the more quickly. It is not easy to see sufficient reason for this view. There may have been some who were unaware of the gravity of the crisis. If there were, it is conceivable that a rise in the bank rate would have roused their apprehensions. But it is difficult to believe that such were in a majority either as regards numbers or as regards possessions. The Continental holders of balances knew that the situation was grave. That was why they were withdrawing their money. And one of the main reasons why they thought it to be grave was the belief that steps would not be taken to raise the rate and contract credit. It is hard to believe that, if they had seen such measures actually taken, they would have been made more apprehensive. No doubt much would have depended upon the time at which these things were done. It may well be that, by the end, the situation had become uncontrollable. But if at the time when foreign assistance was first sought there had been a stiff rise in the rate, it is at least arguable that it would have been effective. The foreign credits would then have appeared as a *mass de manœuvre* available for meeting bear attacks in a manner with which M. Poincaré had made Continental operators familiar. As it was, they must have appeared merely as a means of avoiding credit contraction. Hence they actually functioned merely as a means for the safe repatriation of foreign capital.

A new Government was formed. The Budget was balanced. But there was no rise in the bank rate. The run continued. The last straw was a rumour of a naval mutiny, greatly exaggerated in the Continental newspapers. On September 21st, the right to draw gold from the Bank of England was suspended. Great Britain had left the Gold Standard. To the end the rate of discount was $4\frac{1}{2}$ per cent.

7. Thus ended the post-war Gold Standard as an international monetary system. From this moment the world was broken up into a series of competing local monetary areas, some still on gold, some pursuing different policies of their own. Before dealing with these it is worth while looking back for a moment at the period which had thus ended, and trying to get its main lessons in proper perspective.

The post-war monetary reconstruction was not a success. Its stability was never great and it ended in chaos. It is often said that this failure was inherent in its nature—that the experience of these years shows the Gold Standard as such to be a generator of instability. It was on the Gold Standard that the American boom was generated, it is urged. It was adherence to the Gold Standard which was responsible for the economic difficulties of Great Britain. It was the Gold Standard which engendered this great mass of floating balances which eventually brought the whole structure to disaster. Experience is conclusive against the Gold Standard.

But, if the analysis of the present and earlier chapters is correct, this conclusion is unwarranted. For none of these difficulties can the Gold Standard as such be held responsible. The American boom, as we have seen, was generated on a declining gold basis. The English disequilibrium was the result of the choice of a wrong parity and of failure to conform to its requirements. The floating balances, in so far as they were a special danger, were the product partly of the instability which preceded the restoration of the Gold Standard—the flight from the franc— partly of the persistence of the British disequilibrium. In so far as the disaster of this period is to be attributed to monetary causes, it was not conformity to the logic of the Gold Standard, but rather disregard of this logic, which was at the root of the trouble. It was not the Gold Standard as such but rather the way it was mismanaged, and the peculiarly perilous nature of the environment in which the mismanagement took place, which was the cause of the difficulty; not the Gold Standard, but the choice of a wrong parity and the attempt to work the Gold Standard on managed currency lines, which were responsible for the *débâcle*.

There are, however, certain positive lessons which flow from this recent experience. Two in particular are conspicuous.

In the first place, it is clear that monetary disturbances are likely to be much more severe than would otherwise be the case if they are accompanied by international disequilibrium. Booms and slumps are likely to take place as a result of monetary causes—in the sense defined above—under almost any system, but they are likely to be much more severe if they are the

outcome of the failure of the leading monetary centres
of the world to keep properly in step with one another.
It is almost certain that the extravagance of the
American boom was, in part at any rate, a by-product
of the British disequilibrium. If we had been in equilibrium with the rest of the world it is still unlikely
that the boom would have been avoided; but it is also
improbable that the peculiar distortions which accompanied it would have been present, nor would the
position during the slump have been latent with such
explosive properties.

It follows therefore that, if relative stability is
desired, international equilibrium is a major objective
of policy. But—and here is the second lesson of this
experience—it is clear that this international equilibrium cannot be secured under the Gold Standard
unless the authorities in the various monetary centres
are prepared to work the Gold Standard on Gold
Standard lines. That is to say, they must be prepared
to allow the gold movements to produce their full
effect through the whole system. You cannot work a
local Gold Standard on "managed currency" lines.[1]
This is made abundantly clear by British experience.
No one will wish lightly to pass adverse judgment on
the eminent and disinterested men who gave such
unremitting labour to the conduct of the monetary
policy of Great Britain during these troubled times.
Viewed even from the distance of two short years, the
whole episode assumes more and more the aspects of
a tragedy, a tragedy in which judgments of praise or
blame are equally inappropriate. But in respect of the
actual implications of the policy they pursued, the

---

[1] This does not in the least preclude concerted measures throughout the
world to damp down general fluctuation. See below, pp. 169-172.

verdict of Sir Josiah Stamp, himself a director of the Bank of England, must be taken as final:

> The charge often made by continental writers that the responsibility for working the gold standard throughout the industrial organism was not recognised, must be admitted to be in part true. The gold standard certainly presupposes that the flow of gold to balance international trade must work out its effects in raising and lowering costs; otherwise that standard is meaningless. The gold was flowing for political reasons and other reasons that were artificial compared with the balance of trade, and every effort was made to prevent wages and other costs rising and falling. The natural reactions of the gold standard were, therefore, denied—denied no doubt, or prevented, in self-protection, but all the same having the effects of *prevention* in destroying the self-balancing qualities of the gold standard.[1]

This is a hard saying, and its implications are even harder. Rigidity of costs is inimical to the successful working of an international standard, and for this reason many have been led to seek relief in the device of independent national currencies. Before we can pass judgement on plans of this sort, however, we must examine their operation in practice. But this leads to the subject of the next chapter.

[1] *Economic Essays in Honour of Gustav Cassel*, p. 601.

CHAPTER VI

1. THE abandonment of the Gold Standard by Great Britain meant the end, for the time being at any rate, of the international monetary system. Henceforward the course of the depression in different centres varied with the fortunes of the local monetary system, the disunity itself giving rise to new complications and disturbances. It is the task of this chapter to outline the most conspicuous features of this period of monetary chaos.

2. It is convenient to start with Germany. For the crisis first became acute in Germany. And there are certain special features of the German situation which are deserving of separate comment.

The Germans did not abandon the Gold Standard. Officially at any rate, when the Berlin banks were reopened, the mark was still on a gold basis. For this there were obvious reasons. The memory of inflation dies hard. At the first sign of an official abandonment of the Gold Standard there can be little doubt that the mark would have become almost worthless. The population to a man would have sallied into the shops and bought anything rather than keep money. There would have been a flight into commodities.[1] It is said

___

[1] Whether this would happen now if *Unser Führer* in his wisdom decided to put Dr. Feder's plans into operation, is another question. Perhaps inflation is only conceived to be possible when there are Jews about. When there are good Aryans behind the counter prices do not rise!

that agreements existed between the big concerns and the trade unions that the moment the mark ceased to be on a gold basis all dealings should be calculated in dollars. No doubt this sounds childish to Anglo-Saxons, who do not know yet what a major inflation is. But the burnt child dreads the fire.

Moreover, quite apart from this psychological obstacle there were stubborn mechanical reasons why a depreciation was not thought to be advisable. The overwhelming proportion of the German debts were contracted in gold terms. A depreciation of the exchange would have had the effect of increasing the burden of interest. In those days, at any rate, there seems every reason to suppose that the German authorities honestly intended to make every effort in their power to continue paying their debts. They looked forward to a time when new credits might be desirable. They entertained no desire for retreat into a complete state of self-sufficiency. In such circumstances, and with such objectives, an abandonment of the Gold Standard would have only increased their difficulties.

But the Gold Standard was not maintained in substance. The façade was there. But the machinery ceased to function. To maintain this façade there was erected the most formidable apparatus of exchange control yet known to economic history. The accumulated knowledge of the inflation period was mustered in the Reichsbank to elaborate a mechanism which should make unofficial dealing in foreign exchange, if not impossible, yet so hedged about with penalties and inspection as to reduce it to what have probably been smaller proportions than those prevailing at any earlier period. It is not impossible to get money out of Germany on a small scale. But large-scale evasion of the control is said to be almost out of the question.

Now it may be possible to control the exchange by measures of this sort. But it is not possible to control the number of bills coming forward. That is a matter which depends upon the volume of transactions effected. And it is the paradox of measures of this sort that the more efficient they are from the technical point of view, the more inimical they are to the restoration of trade equilibrium. As an emergency measure against a flight of capital caused by purely political disturbances they may on occasion be effect-ive, though it is arguable that there are almost always alternative measures which would meet the situation more efficiently. But as a cure for less transitory dis-turbances, be it an adverse turn of the terms on which the country in question can do trade or a change of disposition on the part of domestic and foreign capi-talists in regard to the location of their investments, they tend to be self-frustrating. By keeping up the rate of exchange and apparently obviating the necessity for credit contraction, they prevent that expansion of exports which is necessary to restore equilibrium. And the longer such restrictions last, the more rapid is the rate of accumulation of deferred payments. Sooner or later the controlling authorities are forced to take other measures—repudiation of foreign debts, surreptitious subsidies to export and so on. The exchange control in Germany has been more efficient than anything of its kind before, and at the outset the case for its imposition must have seemed almost overwhelm-ing. But it is no accident that German exports have lost ground and that the position of the foreign debtors of Germany to-day is less hopeful than at any time before.[1]

The situation in Germany was moreover complicated by the peculiar arrangements made with foreign creditors. In return for exchange control and certain guarantees about internal repayment, the foreign creditors of Germany undertook not to attempt to withdraw their advances. No doubt it was an advantage to the monetary authorities in Berlin to be immune from attempts at withdrawal. But the strict control of exchange which such agreements necessitated, still more the working of the arrangements as regards repayment, were a highly dubious benefit. Funds which would otherwise have left the country accumulated in the blocked accounts, producing a state of false liquidity peculiarly damaging to money rates as a guide to rational investment. The insistence of the foreign creditors that they should share in all repayments by home debtors produced a situation in which home debtors were even compelled by the banks to defer the repayment of credits in order that the volume of foreign repayments might not be "unduly" augmented. The result was naturally an almost complete paralysis of investment of any kind —a paralysis which was all the more damaging in that it hit sound concerns even more severely than the unsound. Concerns which could have repaid all that they owed were prevented from doing so. Concerns which had no hope of repaying were kept alive. The result was, as might have been expected, deflation and an intensification of the depression.

[1] It is perhaps worth noting that this diagnosis is not a case of wisdom after the event. The substance of this section is adapted, with very little alteration, from a memorandum written in conjunction with a friend for private circulation in the early summer of 1932.

The whole episode is peculiarly instructive. It typifies in a particularly vivid way that new mode of dealing with economic diseases to which allusion was made in an earlier chapter. The fact is that much of the money advanced to Germany was lost, and lost irretrievably. The right way to have dealt with such a situation was to have recognised this—to have examined each case on its merits, to have wound up the bad concerns, written off the bad debts and started anew on a fresh basis. But this was not done, and has not been done even now. Instead, a system was erected which treated good and bad debts indiscriminately, and perpetuated a state of uncertainty and maladjustment in the capital market which had the effect of causing still further deterioration in the general economic position.

In all this the foreign creditors were by no means without responsibility. No doubt the breathing-space thus afforded gave certain influential houses which had over-lent, the opportunity of retrenching in other directions and steadying their position. But the safeguarding of the credit of individual lenders, however important, seems a high price to pay for a prolongation of the general paralysis which was probably the immediate occasion for political changes which have already destroyed all Liberal institutions in Germany, and may yet be responsible for even graver political complications.

3. The abandonment of the Gold Standard by Great Britain was attended by no internal disaster. Having kept the bank rate at $4\frac{1}{2}$ per cent when they were struggling to keep on the Gold Standard, the authorities decided that it was worth while putting it up to 6 per cent now we were off. This obviated any

immediate danger of inflation and tended to restore confidence. By February it was thought safe to lower it to 5 per cent and henceforward by stages to 2 per cent at the end of June. The dollar-sterling exchange rapidly fell to about 3·85, and later in the year it moved down to a lower level in the neighbourhood of 3·40. But for reasons which we shall have occasion to discuss later on, there was no great rise in prices. In September 1931 the level of sterling prices was 99. Three months later (December 1931) it was 106. From September 1931 to September 1933 it only moved between 99 and 103.[1]

But what of the external position? How did the change affect Great Britain *vis-à-vis* the rest of the world? This is a matter of some complexity which it is necessary to examine carefully.

In foreign eyes the abandonment of the Gold Standard by Great Britain was the equivalent of default. In less troubled times the loss of prestige would have been enormous. The chief centre of international finance was not paying twenty shillings in the pound. It is important not to under-estimate the effects of all this on the absolute level of confidence throughout the world. We may be quite sure that in future banks and financial institutions will be much less willing to hold balances in foreign centres. The restoration of the Gold Standard on Gold Exchange Standard lines will be a matter of much greater difficulty than it was before. For good or for bad, the tendency for each Central Bank to accumulate its own reserves of gold has been immensely strengthened.

But actually the relative position of Great Britain has not suffered greatly. Once off the Gold Standard,

---

[1] Board of Trade Index (1913 = 100). See Statistical Appendix, Table 5.

the policy of the Treasury and the Bank has been one of great prudence. The Budget has been balanced. The expansion of credit has been kept within limits. It is true that they have refrained from taking any steps towards a return to gold when it has been arguable that such steps would have contributed greatly to a stabilisation of world conditions. They have left the rest of the world in great uncertainty concerning the future of sterling. But in the face of what at times has been an almost overwhelming pressure to indulge in inflationary experiments, they have pursued a policy of solvency and restraint. Moreover external conditions have altered. As the result of causes, whose operation we shall examine later, the position of other financial centres has weakened. A balance in London, although exposed to the fluctuations of the sterling exchange, has on occasion seemed relatively safer than a balance in most other centres—a *pis aller* no doubt, but, so far as the relative strength of sterling has been concerned, effective for all that.

The fall of the exchange meant a diminution of power to buy foreign products. It is true that, in the event, the prices of some foreign products fell so that the absolute volume of such products purchasable with a pound sterling was not greatly diminished. But it is clear that it is less than it would be if the rate of exchange were higher. No one who has had occasion for foreign travel in the last two years will deny a not inconsiderable impoverishment.

In the same way it has involved a relative shrinkage in the real value of all debts owing to Great Britain and payable in sterling. This is a sacrifice inevitably bound up with the abandonment of the Gold Standard, yet in no way contributory to the solution of the problem which the abandonment of the Gold Standard may be regarded as an attempt to solve. To relieve the over-valuation of the pound and to get into international equilibrium it was necessary either to reduce costs or lower the exchange. The fall of the exchange viewed in this light is simply an automatic instrument for reducing the price of exports and the power to buy imports. But whereas the direct reduction of costs would have left the real value of our sterling assets unaffected, the fall of the exchange has also the effect of surrendering part of such assets. It may be argued that default on such payments was inevitable with the exchange at its former level, and that the fall in the exchange may therefore be regarded as a rough-and-ready arrangement with our debtors. It is certainly true that it has eased the position of such people and, to that extent, may even have been conducive to their recovery. But it is open to the objection applicable to so many of the policies of the slump that it sacrifices good debts along with bad, and most certainly sets a precedent likely to be damaging to the prospects of prudent international lending.

But it is a relief from over-valuation. Here too it may well be objected that it is a crude method of dealing with a very complex question. As has already been emphasised, the maladjustments which were responsible for the disequilibrium in Great Britain were not of that simple order which would be typified by a state of affairs in which all money incomes were a certain percentage too high. They were much more complex than that. The fundamental obstacle to the smooth working of the equilibrating forces was not the height of the various cost items but their rigidity. The depreciation of the exchange removes none of this. It applies a crude cut to the gold value of all sterling incomes. It leaves their relations unaltered and their rigidity unaffected. Indeed it sets a certain seal of inviolability on such arrangements. If we were prepared to abandon the Gold Standard with all the fateful consequences which that involved, rather than change nominal incomes, under what circumstances would such changes be deemed obligatory? Yet it is improbable that the necessity for adaptation to external change ceased in 1931. We may yet pay dearly for our refusal to adopt what from the internal and short-run point of view may well seem to have been the harder alternative.

None the less, the fall of the exchange was a definite relief. By itself it did not, and it could not, remedy the internal disequilibrium—the maladjustment between demand for and supply of the various kinds of labour, and the many other circumstances making for lack of profits and depression. But it did mean that no longer were the export trades to struggle against the burden of an exchange out of relation to a level of costs which seemed unyielding. It did mean that, in so far as the internal disequilibrium was conditioned by external factors, its occasion would be removed. It meant further that, in so far as the exchange fell below its equilibrium point, for the time being it conferred on British exporters a comparative, though of course necessarily transitory and in part self - frustrating, advantage.

How far this happened it is quite impossible to say with any great degree of precision. We do not know the degree of over-valuation which existed when the Gold Standard was abandoned, and we cannot know how the equilibrium relationship has changed since that time. The purchasing-power parity of the foreign exchanges is essentially a doctrine which is only capable of affording quantitative guidance when few elements in the situation are changing. But this has not been the case in the period under discussion. The whole framework of international trade has undergone, as it were, a continuous earthquake. The changes in the channels of trade have been so multitudinous that we can really form no precise idea of the probable volume of trade in more settled conditions. Moreover, the price-changes to which we refer in any attempt to ascertain the changes in the purchasing-power parities are themselves of a kind which is highly unstable. There can be no doubt, as we shall see in detail later on, that some part, at any rate, of the fall in gold prices during this period is to be attributed to the effects of the fluctuations in the exchanges. What value, then, can be attributed to it as a measure of the change in exchange rates which might be expected if exchange rates were relatively stable?

Nevertheless on the crudest tests a considerable degree of under-valuation seems probable. If we assume that the dollar-sterling exchange was 10 per cent over-valued at the time of the departure from gold, the equilibrium rate would have been in the neighbourhood of 4·42. The actual rate in the next four weeks was in the neighbourhood of 3·90. By October 1932 gold prices had fallen from 70 to 64, while sterling prices had only moved from 104 to 101. This means a lowering of the purchasing-power parity calculated on this basis from 4·42 to 4·16. But the actual exchange stood at about 3·40. This probably greatly under-estimates the true under-valuation. A tariff had been imposed on the importation of goods into Great Britain. This must have had the effect of a not inconsiderable raising of the equilibrium exchange rate. Moreover the level of gold prices was clearly abnormal. Given greater stability of conditions it was bound to recover considerably. This diagnosis is in conformity with what appears to be the common experience of merchants and travellers. The fall in the exchange made sterling abnormally cheap.

But there was no immediate response in the figures of external trade. In October 1931 British exports were £32,832,000. By October 1932 they were only £30,440,000. Despite the enormous exchange advantage there had been no important improvement. To understand why this was, we must turn our attention once more to conditions overseas.

4. When Great Britain left the Gold Standard her example was rapidly followed by a number of other countries who, by a number of obscure devices, contrived to depreciate their exchanges to keep more or less in step with the depreciation of sterling. Some, such as Australia, Argentina and Brazil, had abandoned it before. The following chart shows the varying relation to the old gold parity of a representative group of national currencies during this period.[1]

To the extent to which this was not brought about by measures involving a (relative) rise in costs, such depreciation involved for these countries too, for the time being, a relative advantage to trade of the kind we have discussed already.[2] Any pressure to internal contraction was transferred to the exchange market.

---

[1] For the figures on which it is based see Statistical Appendix, Table 36.

[2] Whether the advantage was permanent or not depended upon the extent to which there had previously existed real over-valuation of the currency. If this were not the case, then necessarily the measures taken to depress the exchange must in the long-run wipe out the advantage of depreciation.

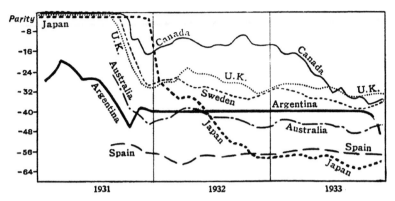

FOREIGN EXCHANGE RATES
Percentage Discount in relation to Gold Parity

The depreciation of the exchange gave a bonus to exporters.

But in the Gold Standard countries there continued a most catastrophic deflation. In September 1931 the index of wholesale prices in the United States stood at 71; by February 1933 it had fallen to 60—a fall of 15 per cent. At no period during the slump had the fall been more extensive or more damaging.

We have examined already the general causes which were making for deflation during the earlier stages of the depression. These causes did not cease to operate. But from September 1931 they were reinforced by new tendencies—the results of the crisis of 1931. A substantial part of the deflation of 1931–32 must be directly attributed to the break-up of the Gold Standard.

At first sight this verdict may appear highly paradoxical. The abandonment of the Gold Standard involved a diminution of the demand for gold as a backing for the currencies concerned. Surely this should imply tendencies the reverse of deflationary in the Gold Standard countries? The argument is plausible—if we think only of the long-run. In the long-run, if this country and others remain off the Gold Standard and other things remain unchanged, there seems reason to suppose that the value of gold will be less than it would otherwise have been—that the general level of gold prices will be higher than it would have been if the area of monetary use of gold had been greater. The precedent of silver seems to bear out this conclusion. The same volume of metal concentrated in a smaller area will surely give rise to a higher level of prices.

The argument is plausible. If we could assume that other things would remain unchanged for a sufficient period, no doubt the results predicted would come about. But the impact effects of a change of the kind we are considering are not of this order; and if the change is on a large scale, they may produce new changes in the situation which postpone almost indefinitely the working out of the long-run tendencies. In the short run the effects of such a change are likely to be highly deflationary. We can best see why this is so if we examine what actually happened.

The suspension of gold payments in London and the fall of the exchange which followed meant a substantial shrinkage in the gold value of all foreign balances which had not already been withdrawn. The immediate effect of this was violently deflationary. Central Banks which had kept part of their reserves in the form of sterling assets suddenly found their reserves depleted in circumstances when the probability of unexpected withdrawals was greater than ever before. It is said that the Bank of France lost a sum exceeding the whole value of its paid-up capital. The Bank of the Netherlands openly announced a loss of over 30 million guilders.

All those smaller Central Banks which had been recon-
structed, often with the advice of British experts, on the
assumption that a sterling balance was as good as gold,
suffered losses of comparable proportions. Nor were
other financial institutions which had abstained from
participating in the general panic in any better position.
Their assets, too, had lost 20 per cent of their value
overnight. One and all commenced a desperate struggle
for liquidity—a struggle which, by its very nature, was
deflationary in its incidence. When the reserve falls
and attempts are made to re-establish liquidity, it is
active investment which suffers.

But this was only the beginning of the trouble. The
struggle for liquidity was not confined to financial
institutions. The fall of the exchange which conferred a
benefit upon British exporters imposed a corresponding
disadvantage on their competitors in foreign markets
whose exchange had not also fallen. The German textile
manufacturer, the Polish mine-owner, the American
car exporter, all found their capital committed to lines
of enterprise in which its value had fallen. Naturally
they, too, commenced to struggle for liquidity—to
shorten credit, to diminish reinvestment, to save what
they could from the wreck.

Nor was this all. The commodity markets were more
directly affected. The fall in the sterling exchange
meant a diminution in demand from buyers whose
capital was in sterling. Now the demand from such
sources in many cases constituted an important proportion of the total demand in the market. A diminution of such demand therefore meant a substantial fall
in gold prices. This fall, in turn, while it permitted the
British consumer to escape any big rise in sterling
prices, meant a further destruction of capital and a

further intensification of the struggle for liquidity. These are things which to-day he who runs may read. Yet at the time they first began, in this country at any rate, whoever ventured to predict them, however *pianissimo*, wrote himself down as perverse and obscurantist—out of touch with the best tendencies of modern thought, unsympathetic to the economics of the new era, enthralled in the tangles of the gold superstition, etc. etc. etc.

All this followed from the effects of the first fall of the exchanges. But these effects were now to be reinforced by policy. The Governments and the Central Banks in the countries remaining on the Gold Standard were composed of men educated in a strong mercantilist tradition. It was not to be expected that they should be content to meet the shrinkage in their respective trade balances due to the tendencies just described, by straightforward contraction of credit. Moreover, if they had, an electorate still more strongly innoculated with similar views would have set other men in their places. Accordingly the various mercantilist expedients were once again adopted. Tariffs, exchange restrictions, quotas, import prohibitions, barter trade agreements, central trade-clearing arrangements—all the fusty relics of mediaeval trade regulation, discredited through five hundred years of theory and hard experience, were dragged out of the lumber-rooms and hailed as the products of the latest enlightenment. Protest, in the few cases in which it was made, was completely unavailing. "You cannot put the clock back", it was said.

It is difficult to exaggerate the state of confusion in international trade which has been produced by these arrangements. We have examined already the effects of tariffs. But if we are to retain a sense of proportion, it must be realised that, in these recent developments, tariffs have been a relatively minor obstacle. It is the exchange restrictions, the quota regulations, the import prohibitions, which have done the greater damage. And it should be added, it is the persistence of such measures which offers the greater obstacle to recovery. Given stability of tariff conditions, however high the rates, the currents of trade may be expected eventually to become adapted to the new situation. The existence of a tariff is not inimical to the achievement of trade equilibrium—although no doubt the equilibrium which may be achieved in this way may be judged by commonly accepted standards to be inferior to that which could have been achieved in its absence. But with these other measures it is different. We have examined already how exchange restriction prevents the restoration of equilibrium. The same thing is true, although for different reasons, of the quotas. When the volume of goods that is permitted to pass the customs' barriers is rigidly fixed and cannot fluctuate with price or exchange fluctuations, then the entire mechanism of international equilibration, be it by way of gold flows or of exchange movements, is thrown completely out of gear. It is sometimes thought that it can be replaced by a series of barter trade agreements. But this is a pure delusion, based on the mistaken belief that equilibrium in the balance of trade between one country and the rest of the world implies equality of exports and imports between it and any other single country. As soon as it is realised that this is only the case by pure accident, the hope of reconstructing trade equilibrium by a series of bilateral agreements is seen to be quite without foundation. The concept of barter

equilibrium is applicable only to exchange between
two groups.

To this chaos there was added yet a further source
of confusion: the fluctuations of exchange. As we have
seen already, when the Gold Standard broke up in
1931, the exchange rates of the centres which abandoned it did not fall to a certain point and then remain
fixed; they continued to fluctuate over a very wide range
(see chart p. 111 above). In December 1931 the pound
sterling had fallen to 3·37. By April it had risen to
3·75. In August it stood at 3·47. By December it had
fallen to 3·27. The fluctuations in other exchanges were
of a similar order of magnitude.

The uncertainty created by these fluctuations was
in itself highly deflationary. It was deflationary in its
effects on day-to-day trade. If there exists a free forward market in foreign exchange it is possible to some
extent for the trader to insure himself against exchange
fluctuations. But it was one of the objects of the
measures already described to prevent free dealing
in the exchanges. Over the area where exchange restriction prevailed, therefore, this expedient was not
available. And in the centres which remained free, a
wide forward market was not always operative. The
volume of trade therefore tended further to contract.

But beyond this, the uncertainty of the exchange
meant an almost complete cessation of long-term international investment. If it is possible to effect an insurance of day-to-day trade and finance, it is out of the
question to carry out any similar operation for long-
term investment. There is no forward market in bonds
and debentures. Either lender or borrower has to take
the risk. If the exchange is fluctuating, therefore, a
considerable curtailment of foreign investment is in-

evitable. If it fluctuates widely, foreign investment is likely to cease. But cessation of foreign investment in a world which has been organised on the expectation of a large volume of capital movement is in itself a deflationary influence. In circumstances of uncertainty, such as we have just described, this influence was likely to be greatly enhanced. An investor in a Gold Standard country was on the horns of a dilemma. He was reluctant to invest at home because he did not know what new damage the exchange was likely to do to domestic industry. The only way out was to refrain from investing. But this meant a continuance of deflation.

In all these ways the break-up of international monetary unity aggravated the difficulties of the countries which still remained on gold. It is not surprising, therefore, that for many months after it had happened the position of the countries which had been eased by the breakdown showed such scanty signs of improvement. Whether or not it be welcomed as a solution for certain very pressing domestic problems, no really impartial observer of world events can do other than regard the abandonment of the Gold Standard by Great Britain as a catastrophe of the first order of magnitude. Will European democracy in the form we have known it survive the repercussions it has engendered? It is much too early to say. But the question is not irrelevant.

It is sometimes said that the dislocation was inevitable, that, given the initial disequilibrium in which Great Britain was placed at the beginning of the slump, similar results must have followed any measures which eliminated it. Whether we adopted the method of cost reduction or the method of releasing the exchange, it was the same thing so far as the rest of the world was concerned, it is urged. From the domestic point of view the adoption of the latter eliminated all the horrors of disputes between capital and labour.

Such a view seems based upon complete misapprehension. It may be admitted that the elimination of our disequilibrium by internal contraction would have caused some disturbance. It would certainly have meant a disadvantage to the foreign manufacturers and miners who competed with our exports. It would have involved some contraction of our demand for imports. But to argue that the probable effects of such measures can be compared with the effects of the abandonment of the Gold Standard is surely to lose all sense of proportion. They would have involved no diminution of the value of foreign balances. They would have involved not the slightest probability of undervaluation of sterling. They would have involved no persistent uncertainties of trade. Suppose that in the spring of 1931 there had been cuts in wage rates in Great Britain of the order of 10 per cent—to take a figure which was often quoted at that time— is it really to be supposed that this could have given rise to the crop of exchange restrictions, tariffs, quotas, and all the other obstacles to trade which frantic Governments elsewhere erected against exchange depreciation? There would have been some gain of competitive advantage by Great Britain. There might have been some competitive wage reductions elsewhere. But in general people would have known where they were. They would have been sure that there was a bottom to this kind of contraction—and with a good deal of grumbling and some obstruction no doubt they would have accepted the result. But with the exchange there was no such certainty. With a depreciating exchange nothing was certain—not even the number of exchange rates which could remain relatively stable. It is impossible that domestic contraction could have led to the same results as competitive depreciation.

5. This brings us to a new phase of the post-crisis chaos.

In the summer of 1932 there began a small revival of business. The orgy of trade restrictionism which had followed the crisis of the previous autumn had begun to abate its intensity. In Great Britain the effects of the fall in the exchange and the restoration of financial solvency were beginning to make themselves felt. In other parts of the world, liquidation and cost-cutting had reached a stage at which the restoration of profitability at some not too far distant date seemed a legitimate expectation. The conclusion of what seemed to be a definitive settlement of the Reparation problem at Lausanne gave a stimulus to confidence. There was a stock exchange recovery. The indices of trade and production turned slightly upwards. For Great Britain and for many other parts of the world this was the beginning of revival.

But in the Gold Standard countries the position was still very precarious. The revival in other parts was to some extent the result of undervaluation of the exchange. The position of those who had maintained continuity of standard was therefore bound to be less favourable. And the continued uncertainty of the exchange was further cause of difficulty. In the autumn, partly as a result of the usual seasonal pressure, partly as a result of apprehensions regarding default on the American debt, partly as a result of the credit expansion which had accompanied the conversion operations, sterling began to fall. In October it stood at 3·39. By December it had fallen to 3·27. Even when apprehension of default had passed, it did not rise above 3·43 until after the American crisis.

In no country was this felt more severely than in the United States of America. The banking situation in that country had long been profoundly unhealthy. The strain of two years of deflation had produced panic psychology on the part of depositors. Especially in the middle west, the banks were loaded up with mortgages, the value of which was probably never fully recoverable. As the international uncertainty continued, gold hoarding became more and more prevalent. Only a revival of confidence could avert a big disaster.

In these circumstances a desperate bid was made from Washington. An unofficial *ballon d'essai* was launched across the Atlantic. If Great Britain would stabilise the pound, it was hinted, then the United States would be prepared to write off a substantial slice of the war debt.[1]

Could anything have been more attractive? Here was the pound sterling almost certainly under-valued, but deprived of the opportunity of conferring the maximum stimulus to recovery by continued uncertainty about its future. Here was the offer, or suggestion of an offer, that in return for taking a step so much to our advantage we should receive the further considerable benefit of a revision of our obligations. Was it ever given to a great nation before in such wise to be bribed into sanity?

But in vain. The antagonists of the Gold Standard, the reflationists, had done their work too well. Go back to the Gold Standard under circumstances quite

---

[1] See the *Economist*, vol. cxvi., Jan. 21, 1933, p. 113.

as favourable as those under which the French went back in 1927—an under-valued exchange and a large margin for a cautious credit expansion? Never. Not until the price-level is at the 1929 (or the 1924) figure, until tariffs have been swept away and all obstacles to trade removed. Sentiments of this sort were voiced freely by the highest authorities. It did not seem to occur to these gentlemen that obstacles to trade would not be removed until the exchanges were stable, that an alleviation of the paralysing instability of the exchanges would have been conducive to a considerable recovery of prices—a recovery which, unlike a return to the 1929 price-level, would not necessarily carry with it the dangers of inflation and collapse—and that the perpetuation of the uncertainty with regard to the future of sterling was creating a position in which resort to competitive depreciation was more and more probable.

Thus the opportunity for a restoration of international stability under conditions of maximum advantage for the ossified cost structure of Great Britain was rejected. It is unlikely to recur.

Meanwhile the position of the American banks was rapidly deteriorating. Uncertainty with regard to future monetary policy, alarm at the revelations of weakness in unsuspected quarters which followed the publication of the Reconstruction Finance Corporation's accounts, the paralysis of business almost inevitable in a change of political régime, had produced an atmosphere of distrust which only needed a very slight jolt to degenerate into complete panic. The jolt came in the shape of a run on the banks of Detroit. A bank holiday was declared in Michigan. The panic spread. Other states followed suit. On March 4th,

1933, when President Roosevelt took up office, the crisis had become general. A general bank holiday was declared and the right to withdraw gold for export was suspended.

The internal crisis was handled with great expedition. An Act was passed giving the President extensive powers to reorganise bankrupt institutions and to regulate the reopening of the sound. An emergency currency was provided. On March 13th such banks as were judged to be sound began to reopen. The Stock Exchange moved upwards.

But the export of gold remained in abeyance and for over a month the position was obscure. There were ample reserves of gold. The trade balance was favourable. To the outside observer, the obvious policy for the President was to proceed as rapidly as possible with the liquidation of the bank crisis and to redouble attempts to stabilise the international position. "There can be little doubt," says the American Institute of Banking, "that at the time the United States departed from the Gold Standard its international economic position was so strong and its own gold holdings so large that no external pressure could easily have forced suspension." [1] But the party that was now in power had other views of policy. Inflationist sentiment, always a strong force in American policy, now became dominant. The advisers of the President were determined to carry through a policy of deliberate reflation. In the pursuance of this policy they conceived that the Gold Standard would prove an obstacle. Accordingly, when the banks reopened, the right to withdraw gold was not restored. By a series of administrative orders culminating in the refusal, on May

[1] *Anti-Depression Legislation*, p. 101.

1st, of licences for the export of gold to meet maturities and interest on United States obligations held abroad, the abandonment of the Gold Standard was confirmed. The dollar-franc exchange at par is 1 dollar = 25·52 francs. In May it was 21·70. Thenceforward it continued to depreciate.

These measures produced a revulsion of opinion in Great Britain. Before the dollar had cut loose from gold, opinion was hostile to any sort of stabilisation. But now things were different. The fear of competitive depreciation was seen to have been no illusion. The advantage of the under-valuation of sterling, which might have been consolidated in a general settlement in February, now seemed likely to be snatched away by still further under-valuation of the dollar. The political repercussions of still further damage to the Gold Standard countries, moreover, were not lightly to be contemplated. If some stabilisation agreement were not reached all hopes of a successful outcome of the World Economic Conference would prove illusory. Something must be done even at this late hour to restore the conditions of stability.

Accordingly when the World Economic Conference met in June, the representatives of the leading Central Banks had established a provisional agreement for stabilisation. So far as Great Britain was concerned the terms were certainly not as good as could have been obtained earlier. Still, such as they were, they were better than nothing. If they could be carried out there seemed good prospect of stabilisation of tariffs and substantial modification of the greater obstacles to international trading. The terms were such as to commend themselves even to the more radical members of the American delegation. To many observers the prospects of sound recovery were present.

But they reckoned without the President. The abandonment of the Gold Standard and the expectation of inflation had produced a minor boom in America. The Dow Jones index of the price of common stocks rose from 59 in April to 92 in July. The prices of raw materials were rising. Any move which set a limit to the prospects of inflation was likely to moderate the pace of the improvement. This was not a prospect which commended itself to the presidential mind. Moreover, he was now set on even more grandiose manœuvres. The Agricultural Adjustment Act, which was to restore prosperity to the farmers (and incidentally to win the Middle West from its Republican allegiance), had declared as an object of policy the raising of prices to the 1926 level, and the restoration of agricultural prices to a pre-war relation to the prices of industrial products. Could this be done on gold? It was doubtful. The President therefore remained recalcitrant and sternly called the assembled nations of the earth to a sense of economic realities.

Thus at one stroke the prospects of stabilisation were shattered. In vain did the reflationists in the President's own team send imploring telegrams to their chief urging him to accept the eminently reasonable settlements they had negotiated. In vain did the redoubtable Professor Moley, hitherto the leader of the American isolationists, bend every nerve to effect a last-minute settlement. It was too late. As on an earlier occasion, it had been easier to bamboozle a President than to debamboozle him. The period of international chaos passed into a new phase.

CHAPTER VII

1. IT is yet too early to say whether the American emergency legislation will prevent the coming of some degree of recovery. The various measures which have been introduced each work in such different directions. The National Recovery Act raises costs and fosters monopoly. The Agricultural Adjustment Act restricts output and subsidises immobility. The Gold Policy attempts to raise prices by a method which increases the scarcity of gold and imposes the maximum inconvenience on the world at large. The unbalancing of the Budget and the vast expenditures on public works have an inflationary tendency which may well override the various impediments to enterprise created in other directions and engender an inflationary boom— a boom which, if the analysis of earlier chapters is correct, would be likely to be followed by a deflationary collapse. It would be futile to attempt to assess in detail the relative importance of these various and rapidly changing influences. It is more fruitful at this stage, if we are to understand the broad conditions of recovery, to examine the underlying principles of certain proposals for reconstruction. It will be observed that such a discussion has a bearing on certain aspects of the American experiments.

2. We may commence with proposals for restricting hours of labour.

In recent years it has often been suggested that the appropriate cure for the slump is a reduction of hours of labour. The enormous volume of unemployment in manufacturing industry, it is held, is a proof that with modern machine production the amount of work to be done is less than the supply of labour available. In such circumstances unemployment is inevitable unless steps are taken to ration the amount of employment that any one labourer may secure. If this could be done by a general reduction of hours, a great curse would be turned into a great blessing—what would have been unemployment for the part would become leisure for the whole. At one stroke the problem of the depression would have been solved.

Now there can be no doubt that a demand for a given number of man-hours is capable of being spread over a greater or a smaller number of labourers according to the number of man-hours that each labourer supplies. *If labour is bought on an hourly basis, therefore, or if it is rewarded according to the volume of product it produces,* a reduction in the length of time it is permitted to employ any one labourer will in all probability involve an increase in the number of labourers hired. It is by no means certain that the increase will be proportionate—that for instance a halving of the working day will result in doubling of the volume of employment. A change of this sort would in many businesses involve an increase in costs other than direct labour costs, an increase in expenditure on supervision, etc., which would diminish the amount available for the purchase of labour. But, broadly speaking, it is not open to question that the volume of employment could be increased by spending the amount devoted to hiring labour on the purchase of smaller quantities of labour from a larger number of men.

But what does this mean? So far as production is concerned it involves no increase on the existing low level. The "work to be done"—the product to be produced—has been done by a greater number of people. Even if we assume that there is no increase in cost, and therefore no diminution in production, can this be said to be a cure for depression? Has anything been done which involves a revival of industrial output? Clearly not. At best—and to ignore all the disorganisation within particular business units, which such a change would involve, is to make a very generous assumption —the effects of the contraction have been redistributed. And a re-expansion of production has been prevented from taking place.

We can perhaps better appreciate the implications of this if we look at the other side of the picture— the effects on working-class income. It should be abundantly clear from what has been said already that an increase of employment due to a reduction of hours involves diminution in the weekly wages of those already in employment. If a man is paid by piece rates a reduction in the time he is allowed to work means a reduction in his income—though not necessarily a proportionate reduction if his rate of output is greater with a shorter working day; if he is paid by the hour, then a strictly proportionate reduction will occur. This is a well-known feature of organised short time in particular industries. There is nothing to suggest that it could be different if organised short time were general.

But is this what labourers want? In discussions of such proposals appeal is often made to the well-known phenomenon that in the past increasing wealth per head has often been taken out partly in increased leisure. The historical fact is unquestionable, as is, indeed, the probable existence of such a disposition on the part of labourers. If wealth per head were to increase it is probable that hours of labour would be shorter. But such considerations are surely irrelevant to the matter under discussion. If the labourers already in employment wished to "take out" part of their *existing* earning power in leisure—that is, if they wished to exchange part of their incomes for greater leisure—it would be open to them to negotiate. The fact that they do not do so, that it would be necessary to prevent them by law from working as long as they do now, suggests that the adjustment that would be brought about in this way would not be, from their point of view, a movement towards equilibrium.

In fact, of course, the popularity of the proposal we are discussing depends essentially upon the tacit assumption that, if hours were shortened in this way, weekly wages would not be lowered—that is, that the price of labour per hour and piece rates would be adjusted upwards. But if this were the case there is no reason to believe that unemployment would be diminished. For a reduction of hours, weekly wages remaining constant, means an increase in the cost of labour per unit. To employ the *same* number of men as before would cost the same total amount. But unless the daily output per man remained constant—a most improbable outcome of the big reductions usually proposed—the cost per unit of output would increase. There would therefore be an incentive to a contraction of employment. The volume of unemployment would be increased.

It is sometimes alleged that this effect would not follow, since the employers would borrow more from the banks to finance an increase of their wage bill. There seems no reason to believe this to be at all probable, at any rate as a general rule. As a general rule, business men will be disposed to borrow more from their banks when the prospects of profit are increasing. In certain cases when there occurs an unexpected increase in costs which is not expected to be permanent, they may borrow more than usual. But such cases are to be regarded as exceptional. The justification of such borrowing is the transitory nature of the increase. A legislative increase of costs such as is involved by a compulsory reduction of hours, wages remaining constant, does not fall within this category. The net effect of such a measure would be a contraction rather than an increase of borrowing. If in the United States, where, under the National Recovery Act, measures of this sort have been put into operation, there is not an absolute increase of unemployment, this will be because of the simultaneous operation of other tendencies—lavish Government expenditure and the like—which work in the other direction more powerfully. If recovery comes, it will be in spite of these measures, not because of them. In isolation they are inimical both to employment and to production.

3. It is clear then that a general restriction of productive activity offers no hope of escape from depression. We may turn, therefore, to proposals for restriction in limited areas.

The course of the slump, as we have already seen, has been marked by extreme depression in agricultural and raw material production. The industries producing food and raw materials have suffered falls in the prices they receive for their products far greater in magnitude than those taking place at other points of the industrial system. In many quarters, therefore, it has been suggested that concerted measures for the restriction of this kind of output are an essential condition of revival. Only in this way, it is said, can the prices of such products be raised to their old level. Only in this way can a "proper balance" be restored to the world economy. So strong a hold indeed have such views on the minds of certain leaders of opinion that there can be little doubt that the news of widespread earthquakes and inundations, which reduced substantially the total capacity of the world to produce such products, would be hailed by them as a bull point for general recovery. A beneficent interposition of Providence would have performed at a stroke a restoration of the "balance" which a score of international conferences might accomplish much less perfectly.

Such beliefs are founded upon delusion. There is no "proper balance" between one industry and another in the sense of a ratio of prices which must not be changed whatever the changes in the general conditions of production.[1] The fall in prices of food and raw materials is the resultant of two tendencies. Partly it is due to the contraction of demand which is the sign of the downward phase of a general fluctuation. On general grounds we should expect to find the fluctuations of raw material prices much greater than any other. In so far as it is due to this, and to the superimposed deflationary influences we have examined, it is reasonable to expect

[1] The whole notion of a proper balance between industry and industry, of which so much is heard in popular discussion of planning, etc., is relevant only to the sphere of aesthetics or military strategy, if it is not strictly related to considerations of prices and costs. Outside these spheres it is an almost perfect example of the pseudo-concept—a concept which on analysis proves to have no content of meaning.

that to some extent it will be reversed in any recovery of trade. But it is due partly to an intensification of productivity in these branches of production, due, not merely to the influences of the boom, but to the march of technical progress—an intensification of productivity which has encountered a relatively inelastic demand. In so far as it is due to such causes, there is no reason whatever to expect a restoration of the old price ratios. If the products whose prices have fallen relatively are produced in centres from which no migration is possible, then, in the absence of restriction, we should expect a permanent change of the same order as the original fall. The inhabitants of such areas would have lower incomes. The inhabitants of other areas would have more to spend on other things. If they are produced in areas from which migration is possible, then there would come about some shift over to better-paid occupations, which would have the effect of mitigating the original fall.[1] But there is no reason to expect that the old price relationship would be restored.

Now it is conceivable that restriction schemes may have the effect of restoring the old relationship. As we shall see later on, there are very grave difficulties in the way of their successful management. But if they do succeed, they do so merely by depriving those members of the world community who would have gained by greater cheapness of the benefits which the technical changes which brought about the initial price-change have made possible. They are exactly equivalent, if they are successful, to natural disasters which limit productivity; or to a deliberate suppression of technical progress. If they benefit the producers of the commodity restricted, they do so by damaging the

[1] See Chapter II. pp. 15-16, above.

producers of other commodities. And if they become widespread they are apt to recoil with damaging effects even on those who originally benefited. Restriction in one line of production may benefit the restricted. Restriction all round leads to general impoverishment. A rise of prices brought about by restriction in many industries would be an indication not of increased wealth but of increased poverty.

It is sometimes said, however, that such schemes have the effect of restoring purchasing power and in that way promoting recovery. Such contentions are the obverse of the fallacy we examined in an earlier chapter. A change of relative prices of this sort has no direct significance so far as the total volume of spending is concerned. The man who has to pay more for bacon has less to spend on cloth. The pig farmer might borrow more from the bank. But the cloth manufacturer will borrow less. And, as we shall see later, general restriction is probably deflationary.

An apt illustration of all this is provided by American experience. For many years American agriculture has been in chronic difficulties. Ever since the war the prices of agricultural products have been tending downwards. In June 1920 the price of No. 2 winter wheat in Chicago was 295 cents per 60 lb. In June 1929 it was 113 cents. The prices of cotton, maize, hogs and other staples have moved, if not with the same rapidity, at least in the same direction. The farmers, many of whom mortgaged their farms in the boom period of 1920, have found it increasingly difficult to meet their obligations. Even when manufacturing industry was booming there was some distress in the agricultural districts. With the coming of industrial depression this distress has become widespread. Many of the most conspicuous features of American political history in the last fifteen years are only to be explained in terms of the influence of the difficulties of the farmers of the South and the Middle West.

In all this there is no particular mystery for the economist. The agricultural experts who provide esoteric explanations in terms of deficiencies of marketing arrangements, shortage of agricultural credit, inadequate diffusion of crop reports and the like, have lost their way in a mass of not very interesting details. They see the fly on the barn door but they do not see the barn door itself. The difficulties of agriculture here, as elsewhere in modern economic history, are to be explained, in the large, in terms of an increase of productivity due to technical progress which encounters a relatively inelastic demand. Superimposed on this are the further difficulties due to the industrial slump—difficulties which, as has been said already, may be expected to disappear if manufacturing industry revives. But, in the main, the secular tendency is clear. Technical progress in American agriculture has been very rapid. The American farmer is feeling with especial force the pressure of those influences which in the course of history have tended continually to reduce the proportion of effort devoted to the production of agricultural staples. In the beginning it was 100 per cent. Since then it has been diminishing. In the absence of restriction, it would in all probability continue to diminish.

In such circumstances there is only one solution which does not involve a deliberate rejection of the fruits of technical progress, or a permanent impoverishment of agricultural producers. A certain proportion of the producers of the products whose prices have fallen must change over to an occupation the demand for whose product is more elastic. There must be a reshuffling of the labour force—a contraction of the proportion employed on the production of products in relatively inelastic demand and an expansion of the proportion employed elsewhere.

Now there can be no doubt that such a process bears hard on particular producers. A change of this sort necessarily involves the breaking of old associations, the rupture of deep-rooted habits. When its incidence is slow, the transfer can come about mainly by a shift of the younger generation. When it is more rapid, or when it has been delayed by State intervention, the propping up of agricultural prices by subsidy and Government buying, more drastic movements are necessary. There can be no doubt that in America the political pressure from the agrarian interests has been tremendous.

But it so happens that in America in recent years there has been ready to hand an expedient which, while fostering no artificial restriction and giving rise to no false hopes for agricultural producers, would have unquestionably done much to ease the difficulties of the transition and to mitigate the pressure on the farmers —a lowering of the industrial tariff. The American farmer has been subject to two pressures—the reduction of his money-income due to the forces we have been discussing, and an increase of costs, a curtailment of markets and a reduction of real income due to the operation of American tariff. This second pressure is in no wise dictated by the operation of consumers' demand or the course of technical progress. It is the direct result of restrictions on division of labour imposed in the interests of manufacturing industry. Its net result, so far as agriculture is concerned, is to make the degree of contraction necessary to bring real incomes into equilibrium greater than would otherwise be the case. A lowering of the tariff would have the effect of extending agricultural markets, lowering agricultural costs, raising agricultural incomes, and to that extent relieving the pressure to contraction.

It would have been reasonable to expect, therefore, that the policy of successive Governments would have been based upon this knowledge. While doing nothing that would hinder the movement from the more depressed branches of agriculture, or raise false hopes of a fundamental change in the direction of secular pressure, a Government determined to give a square deal to agriculture might have been expected to strain every nerve to reduce industrial tariffs—already, as we have seen, a cause of general disturbance and disequilibrium in the world economy as a whole.

But it was not so. We have already examined the effects of Mr. Hoover's policy. The grandiose buying organisations by which he tried to maintain agricultural prices had the effect of demoralising markets altogether, by the accumulation of stocks and the creation of uncertainty. At the same time, by raising false hopes in the minds of the producers, they tended to arrest the contraction of agricultural production.

President Roosevelt has been more thorough. The Agricultural Adjustment Act declares it to be the policy of Congress "To establish and maintain between the production and consumption of agricultural commodities . . . such a ratio as will re-establish prices to farmers at a level that will give agricultural commodities a purchasing power with respect to articles that farmers buy, equivalent to the purchasing power

of commodities in the base period. The base period
. . . shall be the pre-war period, August 1909 to July
1914." To this end it proposes in various ways to restrict production by paying farmers to throw land out
of cultivation. No reduction of tariffs has been carried
through, and the provisions of the National Recovery
Act make it extremely unlikely that any substantial
reduction will take place. It is worth noting that at
the same time under the Tennessee Valley Authority
Act steps are being taken to provide for "the flood
control . . . and the agricultural development of the
said valley".

Thus the net effect of the State intervention in
American agriculture is this. The industrial workers
will pay more for their food (they pay, as it were,
twice—once in the rise of price which restriction brings
about and once in the processing tax by which it is
hoped to subsidise the restriction), and the farmers
continue to pay high prices for industrial products and
suffer the curtailment of markets which is the consequence of industrial protection. At the same time, the
subsidy which they receive for the curtailment of
acreage is a definite incentive to marginal producers
to stay where they are. Presumably when the agricultural development of the Tennessee Valley has been
provided for, there will be more subsidies to keep part
of it out of cultivation.

4. Not all restrictionism is as avowedly restric-
tionist as the Agricultural Adjustment Act The
subtler apologist for the various producers' rings,
pools, marketing boards and the like which, with the
enthusiastic support of the Governments of the world,
are rapidly being brought into being, will defend them,
not on the ground that they restrict sales and produc-

tion, but on the ground that they promote "orderly marketing" and eliminate "wasteful competition". They bring order into the "chaos of unrestricted capitalism". They permit "conscious control" of the fortunes of the various industries. All of which sounds very pleasant. But it is not irrelevant to ask what it means.

"Orderly marketing" means the raising or the maintenance of prices. The various pools and marketing boards which have justified their existence in these terms have all had this object in view and, at the outset of their operations at any rate, have not infrequently succeeded in bringing it about. The more candid supporters of such schemes have been quite frank about this. Let us hear, for instance, Mr. Aaron Sapiro, the founder of the American Pool Movement: "When we go into co-operative marketing activities," he said to the Indiana Wheat Marketing Conference, "do we say we are simply going to try to get some little economy in the handling of wheat? No, because you and I know that we can't handle wheat as far as the physical handling alone is concerned any more cheaply than the big elevator companies. . . . We don't say that the purpose of co-operative marketing is to introduce any economy in the physical handling of grain, because we think that particular point is absolutely too trifling to bother about. What are we trying to do? When we talk of co-operative marketing we say this: We are interested in raising the basic level of the price of wheat." [1]

Such changes are only likely as a result of restriction—restriction of sales and eventually restriction of

[1] Quoted by Boyle, "The Farmers and the Grain Trade", *Economic Journal*, vol. xxxv., 1925, p. 18.

production. It is sometimes urged that the basic price can be raised merely by evening out sales throughout a given crop year. This plea is singularly lacking in substance. In the case of the staple gradeable products, at any rate, there is no reason whatever to suppose that fluctuations within the crop year are not evened out already, so far as this is desirable, by the machinery of the market. Whenever this matter has been investigated by impartial observers the same conclusion has been reached. The supporters of the wheat pool projects, for instance, made much of the contention that wheat "dumping", as they called it, upset the course of prices. The investigations of Professor Boyle and the Leland Stanford Food Institute showed beyond question that this was entirely without foundation.[1] It is quite conceivable, and no doubt very often happens, that an isolated producer, temporarily short of cash, may sell to a local dealer at a price lower than the price he would have obtained if he could have waited a day or two. But quantitatively such cases are not important. In any case they do not demand the setting up of nation-wide monopolies as remedies. In the main there can be no doubt that "orderly marketing", when that stands for marketing schemes making it compulsory for producers to market their products through one central authority, stands also for restriction of production. If it were not so, then it would not be thought necessary to give the organisers of such schemes statutory powers to limit output.

But is not some restriction desirable? The more intelligent supporters of such schemes will admit that

---

[1] Professor Boyle examined the average price of cash wheat in Chicago for forty-three years and found that the total spread for the year was nine cents—barely sufficient to cover carrying charges (*op. cit.* p. 23).

they involve restriction, but only such restriction, they will contend, as is indicated by the demand for the product. If the conditions of demand make it desirable, they will urge, it will be possible to relax the limits of restriction.

To such a contention two answers are possible. In the first place it is surely not irrelevant to point out that an association of producers with statutory powers to exclude competition is not necessarily the best judge of the interest of consumers. Monopolistic bodies without statutory powers may well be restrained from great exploitation of their position by fear of potential competition. It is not so clear that restraint of this sort will dictate the policy of monopolies backed up by State authority. "The interests of dealers in any particular branch of trade or manufactures is always in some respects different from, and even opposite to, that of the public. To widen the market and to narrow the competition is always the interest of the dealers. To widen the market may frequently be agreeable enough to the interest of the public, but to narrow the competition must always be against it and can serve only to enable the dealers by raising their profits above what they naturally would be, to levy, for their own benefit, an absurd tax upon the rest of their fellow citizens. The proposal of any new law or regulation of commerce which comes from this order ought always to be listened to with great precaution, and ought never to be adopted till after having been long and carefully examined, not only with the most scrupulous, but with the most suspicious, attention. It comes from an order of men, whose interest is never exactly the same with that of the public, who have generally an interest to deceive and even to oppress the public, and who accordingly have, upon many occasions, both deceived and oppressed it." [1] Nothing that has happened in the hundred and fifty years since this was written has made it less applicable now than it was then. State-aided monopolies of producers, now as then, are not the best judges of the interests of the consumer.

But even if this were not the case, even if it could be shown that the State-aided monopolist, new style, was a totally different animal from the State-aided monopolist of Adam Smith's day,[2] from the point of view of the consumer there would still be reason for regarding the principles on which he acts with very grave misgiving. The criterion of restricting supply to demand, which is so loudly proclaimed as the object of these schemes, is no criterion at all. There is no such thing as demand for a commodity irrespective of its price. And so long as a price exists at all there is unsatisfied demand for the product. Whether from the consumers' point of view it is more desirable that the demand which is left unsatisfied—excluded that is to say—at any given price, should be supplied before the unsatisfied demands for other commodities are provided for, depends essentially upon the prices of the other commodities and the ability and willingness of labour and capital to migrate from one line to another. From the consumers' point of view, the only justifiable restriction on the supply of one commodity is that which is exerted by the competing demand for others. The only justifiable restriction on the supply of potatoes is the limitation on indefinite transfer into

---

[1] *Wealth of Nations* (Cannan's Edition), vol. i. p. 250.

[2] It does not seem very clever to argue that such a transformation is effected by putting a "representative of the consumer" on the Board of Management.

potato production which is provided after a certain point by the prospects of wages and profits elsewhere. Before this point is reached restriction is damaging to the consumer. Afterwards it is unnecessary.

Now this is not the view of the supporters of State-aided monopoly. For them the underlying principle of restriction—the *rationale* of the mysterious adjustment of supply to demand to which allusion has been made already—is just this, that no expansion shall be permitted which lowers the value of capital already invested in the industry. No doubt most restriction attempts to do more than this—to raise the value of capital already invested in the industry. But this is not an aim to which public appeal is made. The public policy of restrictionism is the maintenance of the value of invested capital.

But this policy is completely at variance with the interests of the consumer. The interest of the consumer, as we have seen, is to get as much of each commodity as is compatible with the service of demand for others. The maintenance of the value of invested capital may very well mean that producers who find prospects in one industry more attractive than the prospects in any others are prevented from entering it, that cost-reducing improvements of technique which would greatly cheapen the commodity to consumers are held up, that the "wasteful competition" of people who are content to serve the consumer for lower returns than before is prevented from reducing prices. Every schoolboy knows that the cheapness which comes from importing corn is incompatible with the maintenance of the value of the corn lands which would be cultivated if import were restricted. The platitudes of the theory of international trade do not lose any of their force when they are applied to domestic competition. The argument, for instance, that road transport diminishes the value of railway capital has just as much and just as little force as the argument that cheap food lowers the value of agricultural property. "To be consistent," said Ricardo, "let us by the same act arrest improvement, and prohibit importation." [1] Economic progress, in the sense of a cheapening of commodities, is not compatible with the preservation of the value of all capital already invested in particular industries. A policy which is directed to this end, therefore, is a policy which conflicts with this conception of economic progress.

But do we want economic progress in this sense? This is clearly a question of ultimate valuation upon which neither economics nor any other science is capable of giving a decision. All that science can do is to present the alternatives. The ultimate decision is one of will, not of knowledge. But, if a digression into this sphere be permitted, it does seem pertinent to observe that the majority of the human race are still very poor and that if, in the interests of a supposed stability, a halt is to be called in the process of raising real incomes, it is an issue which should be squarely presented to those who are most affected by it. It is all very well for the dilettante economists of wealthy universities, their tables groaning beneath a sufficiency of the good things of this world, their garages furnished with private means of transport, to say, "Food is cheap enough. Charabancs are vulgar. The railways are admirable. We have enough of plenty. Let us safeguard security." It is for the millions to

[1] *On the Influence of a Low Price of Corn on the Profits of Stock* (Gonner's Edition), p. 253.

whom a slice of bacon more or less, or a bus ride to the
sea, still matter, to make the decision. It is not so
certain that, if the issue were clearly and honestly explained to them, they would choose the maintenance
of existing capital values. For as yet the issue has not
been put either honestly or clearly.

5. There are certain further aspects of restrictionism which, from the point of view with which we are
especially concerned in this essay, it is particularly
desirable to bear in mind.

The effect of restrictionism, as we have just seen,
is to maintain (or to enhance) the value of capital
already invested in the industry in which production
is restricted. But it does this by lowering the prospective return on capital which is invested elsewhere. If,
before restriction was applied, there was a tendency
for more capital to be invested in the restricting industry—and it is such a tendency which is the *raison
d'être* of restrictionism—it should be clear that when this
channel of investment is closed, other channels where
the prospective return is thought to be lower must be
resorted to. That is to say, the productivity of new
investment is lower. There will be more invested in
other lines of industry than would have been the case
had restriction not been applied. The volume of
workers seeking employment in other lines of industry,
too, will be greater.

Now if investors are not quickly responsive to this
change in the rate of return on investment, the effect
will be a tendency to deflation. And surely this is not
improbable. The man who is prevented from reaping
a gain of, let us say, 7 per cent on investment in road
haulage will not immediately be content with the 6
per cent which is perhaps the best he can hope for

elsewhere. He will say, "Things can't be as bad as all this; I must wait a bit". So he keeps his money on deposit or in some short-dated security. There is a tendency for saving to lag behind active investment—a drag on the velocity of circulation. The proliferation of restriction schemes may preserve existing capital values, but it is detrimental to the revival of investment.

But beyond this, and far transcending it in long-run importance, is the tendency of restrictionism to spread. There is a sort of snowball tendency about this kind of interventionism which has no limit but complete control of all trade and industry. It is clear that, within the restricting industries, the State will be driven to adopt closer and closer control if the schemes are not to break down from evasion of their rules. It is one thing to forbid farmers and others not to produce more than a certain quota. It is another thing to prevent them doing so. The Agricultural Adjustment Act which pays farmers to throw land out of cultivation contains the pathetic proviso that such restriction must be unaccompanied by "increase of commercial fertilisation". How, short of the socialisation of American farming, do the framers of this stipulation propose to put it into force?

But the tendency to extension of control does not operate only within the industries already partially socialised. It works just as conspicuously outside this sphere. As we have seen already, the fact that production in one line is limited means that more capital and labour will be available for other lines of production. The fact that some farmers who wish to grow potatoes are precluded from doing so, because they are not in the original restriction scheme, means that more of other kinds of produce will be forthcoming.

But this increase in supply will bring down prices. The earnings of those already in these lines of production will be reduced. They will go to the Government and say: "You have helped the growers of potatoes to make higher profits, but it is time you did something for us. If you don't, we shall insist that it is a scandal and a shame that we are not allowed to grow more potatoes." There is no law of analytical economics which obliges us to conclude that a minister of agriculture, anxious to make his way in the world, will not tell them to go away and be content with lower earnings. But experience suggests that this is not the line he will adopt. And so new controls are instituted. It is the overwhelming verdict of theory and war-time experience that once Governments start to control important branches of industry, if they are not willing at some point definitely to reverse their whole line of policy, there is no stop to this process short of complete socialism.

6. But is this a tendency we wish to avoid? It is not clear that this is the attitude of the present leaders of opinion. Socialism is a term which is not universally popular. But "planning"— ah! magic word — who would not *plan*? We may not all be socialists now, but we are certainly (nearly) all planners. Yet, if planning is not a polite name for giving sectional advantages to particular industries, what does it denote but socialism—central control of the means of production? A "planned" economy introduced by right-wing parties might for a time (until the parties of the left got control) acknowledge certain rights to the receipt of income, in the past associated with the ownership of property, which would be destroyed at the outset by a purely socialist dictatorship. But, if it were to be true

to its name, it could not acknowledge the substance of ownership, the right of individual disposal of the actual instruments of production. For "planning" involves central control. And central control excludes the right of individual disposal. Nothing but intellectual confusion can result from a failure to realise that Planning and Socialism are fundamentally the same. Now the leaders of opinion want planning.

But do they know what they mean? Have they really faced what planning involves? This is by no means so certain.

It is often thought that the erection of State-aided monopolies of the kind we have discussed already is an integral part of the general policy of planning, and that the problems which confront the framers of such schemes are essentially the problems of a planned society. No doubt this belief is helpful to the interests which benefit from the existence of State-aided monopoly: it enlists for the support of sectional exploitation a body of disinterested opinion which would otherwise be hostile. But it rests on misapprehension. The problems which confront the organisers of a particular industry differ, not only in degree, but also in kind from the problems which confront the organisers of a planned economy.

A simple example should make this quite clear. It is to the interest of any particular branch of industry that it should have plentiful supplies of capital at low rates of interest. Only if the rate of return on new investment in that industry were zero and the rate at which it borrowed were also zero would its interest in more and cheaper capital be at an end. But for the organisers of the system as a whole it presents itself in quite a different manner. For them it is not desirable that any particular industry should have an unlimited claim, at the lowest possible rates, to the limited supply of free capital. For them the problem is essentially a problem of distributing the given supply between different industries. The solution of this problem is different in kind from the solution of the former problem. Long before the organisers of a particular industry would cease to benefit from a reduction of the rate at which they could borrow, there would come a point at which the economy as a whole would lose by not devoting capital to some other object. From the point of view of the economy as a whole, making certain assumptions regarding the relative importance of different consumers, the greatest gain would be reaped when all industries borrowed at an equal rate. From the point of view of any particular industry there would always be a gain in borrowing more cheaply than the others.

It should be clear then that the problem of planning is not to be solved by giving each industry the power of self-government (*i.e.* restriction of entry and production). This is not planning; it is syndicalism. It merely extends to whole industries the right to make plans for themselves similar to the right already enjoyed by individual *entrepreneurs*. But by eliminating competition, or potential competition, it creates a state of affairs much less likely to be stable—much more likely to be restrictive—than the so-called chaos of competitive enterprise. President Roosevelt may think that by suspending the Sherman Act, and by giving each industry the right to restrict competition, he is creating the framework of an ordered society. But he is likely to receive a rude shock. A planned economy must be planned from the centre. This is the only intelligible meaning which can attach to the concept.

7. But on what basis is planning to take place?[1] The *rationale* of a planned society must surely be that it serves some purpose outside the plan. It must be planned for something. There are few who would regard the mere imposition of a pattern as an end in itself. What purpose is the plan to serve? Whose preferences are to govern the organisation of production?

If the question is put in this way the answer seems obvious. A democratic community, at any rate, will attempt to organise production to meet the preferences of consumers. It will not value branches of production as such. It will value them for the various individual satisfactions which they make possible. It will not decide that the production of boots must be a certain absolute volume before it has ascertained the relative strength of the demand for boots and the demand for the products whose production has to be sacrificed if capital and labour are put to this job rather than to others. It will seek to distribute the factors of production between different lines of industry in such a way that it will be impossible to withdraw them from any one line and put them to any other without the products sacrificed being of greater value than the products gained. And if wants change, or if the means of satisfying them alter, it will seek to rearrange production so as once more to attain this end.

But how is this to be done? What mechanism is available for ascertaining the complex and changing tastes of the millions of different individuals constituting the community? And what means are present for

---

[1] The argument which follows owes much to the work of Professor Ludwig von Mises. See especially his *Gemeinwirtschaft*. A translation of this important book is shortly to appear in English.

deciding the relative efficiency of the different factors of production for satisfying these ends? How will the organisers of the planned economy choose between the production of boots and the production of potatoes? And having chosen, how will they decide the most expeditious methods of production?

Let us examine first the ascertainment of the preferences of consumers. It should be quite clear that this is not a matter which can be satisfactorily settled by the methods of political election. The problem of the planning of production concerns a vast multiplicity of alternatives. It is not a matter of "Vote for Jones and more umbrellas" or "Vote for Smith and more waterproof suiting". Thousands of commodities are involved and the possibilities of alternative grouping run into many millions. It is clear that to attempt to solve the problem this way would result in complete chaos—a chaos which would result, not in consumers getting what they wanted, but in their being given simply what the planning authority on quite arbitrary principles decided that they ought to want—which would be by no means the same thing.

At first sight there seems ready to hand a much more efficient mechanism. If the various individuals constituting the community were given sums of money and were left free to bid for the various commodities available, there would result a series of prices which would be the objective register of their various preferences. The market in this respect may be compared to a continuous election with proportional representation. Every shilling spent is a vote for a particular commodity. The system of prices as a whole is the register of such an election.

It might be supposed then that a democratic com-

munity, determined to plan production, would attempt
to resort to the market as a means for ascertaining the
relative urgency of the demand for the various commodities available. A plan which was based upon the
preferences of consumers would seek so to distribute its
productive resources that the demand for all commodities was satisfied to the same level of urgency.
If in making clothes a given quantity of labour
produced less value in price terms than it would
produce in the making of, let us say, fireworks, it
would be withdrawn from the one and devoted to the
other. And so with all the multitudinous instruments
of production.

But it is one thing to sketch the requirements of the
plan. It is another thing to conceive of its execution.
It is in carrying out these requirements of productive
organisation that the project of planning to meet consumers' demands seems likely to encounter obstacles
of a quite fundamental character—obstacles of whose
existence the majority of the advocates of planning do
not seem to have the slightest suspicion.

The requirement of a rational plan, as we have just
seen, is that the factors of production (the land, capital
and labour) should be so distributed between the
various alternatives of production that no commodity
which is produced has less value than the commodities
which might have been produced had the factors of
production been free for other purposes. But how is this
to be carried out? How is the planning authority to
decide what distribution of resources satisfies this requirement? We have seen that it can do something to
ascertain the preferences of consumers by permitting
the pricing of the different commodities they consume.
But clearly this is not enough. It must know also the

relative efficiencies of the factors of production in producing all the possible alternatives.

On paper we can conceive this problem to be solved by a series of mathematical calculations. We can imagine tables to be drawn up expressing the consumers' demands for all the different commodities at all conceivable prices. And we can conceive technical information giving us the productivity, in terms of each of the different commodities, which could be produced by each of the various possible combinations of the factors of production. On such a basis a system of simultaneous equations could be constructed whose solution would show the equilibrium distribution of factors and the equilibrium production of commodities.

But in practice this solution is quite unworkable. It would necessitate the drawing up of millions of equations on the basis of millions of statistical tables based on many more millions of individual computations. By the time the equations were solved, the information on which they were based would have become obsolete and they would need to be calculated anew. The suggestion that a practical solution of the problem of planning is possible on the basis of the Paretian equations simply indicates that those who put it forward have not begun to grasp what these equations mean. There is no hope in this direction of discovering the relative sacrifices of alternative kinds of investment. There is no hope here of a means of adjusting production to meet the preferences of consumers.

Under competitive conditions this problem is solved by a comparison of costs and prices. In a free capitalistic society, the business man, deciding in what line to extend his enterprise, will take two things into consideration: on the one hand, the prices at which various commodities may be expected to sell; on the other, the costs which their production by various technical methods may be expected to incur. His expectations of price are based upon his knowledge of markets. His expectations of cost on technical information coupled with knowledge of the prices for the various factors of production. But the prices of the various factors of production, which are the resultant of the competitive bidding of the different *entrepreneurs*, tend to reflect the value of their contribution to the production of different products. If, therefore, costs are below prices in any line, that is an indication that additions to production in that line are more valuable in terms of consumers' preferences than the things which are being produced elsewhere—that transfer would result in a distribution of factors more in accordance with the preferences of consumers. If, under competitive conditions, the cost of producing potatoes is above the price which potatoes will fetch, that is an indication that some of the resources devoted to producing potatoes would produce things of more value elsewhere. Computations of costs and prices under competitive conditions are, as it were, a short cut to the solution of the millions of equations whose multiplicity we found such an obstacle to planning. The free market does the rest.

But, unfortunately, it is not easy to see how such computations could be made by a planning authority. For the possibility of computations of relative profitability of this sort involves the existence, not merely of a market for final products but also of markets for all the multitudinous elements entering into costs: raw materials, machines, semi-manufactures, different kinds of land, labour, expert guidance and, last but not least, free capital—with the *entrepreneurs* constituting the sellers and buyers, each acting according to his anticipation of the prices in the various markets in which they operate. But, by definition, the central planning authority has abolished all that. It disposes of all resources. There is no division between buyers and sellers. A plan is the centralised disposal of factors of production. And centralised disposal of the factors of production precludes the existence of free markets. The planning authority can order production to be organised how it wishes. But it does not seem to be in a position to keep accurate accounts. How, then, can it plan in the spirit we have postulated?

It is sometimes thought that this difficulty can be surmounted by the creation of fictitious markets. The planned society is to be broken up again into semi-independent productive units, and the management of these units must, as it were, *play* at competition. They will bid against each other for factors of production, sell their products competitively, in short behave *as if* they were competitive capitalists. In this way the planned society will be realised.

There is a certain aesthetic attraction in the contemplation of a project which, setting out to eliminate the institutions of a "planless" society—the "chaos of competitive enterprise"—arrives finally at an attempt to reproduce them. Unfortunately there does not seem reason to suppose that the reproduction would be successful. The propounders of such schemes conceive of the problem in altogether too static and *simpliste* a manner. They conceive of competitive prices as springing from the demands of clearly demarcated administrative units whose continuity can be postulated without destroying the hypothesis that competitive prices are realised. But this is not the case. The conditions of demand and supply are continually changing. Tastes change. Technique changes. The availability of resources and the supply of labour and capital is in process of continual alteration. Competitive prices in the factor markets are the resultant of all this multiplicity of forces influencing the disposal of individual capital. For competition to be free the *entrepreneur* must be at liberty to withdraw his capital altogether from one line of production, sell his plant and his stocks and go into other lines. He must be at liberty to break up the administrative unit. It is difficult to see how liberty of this sort, which is necessary if the market is to be the register of the varying pulls of all the changes in the data, is compatible with the requirements of a society whose *raison d'être* is ownership and control at the centre. No doubt capitalism as we know it, encumbered on all sides by interventionism and State-created monopoly, and distorted by the vagaries of mismanaged money, is very far short of the accuracy of competitive adjustment. But with all its deficiencies in this respect, it seems a much more flexible mechanism than the collectivist alternatives. The path towards a completely planned economy is not a path towards, it is a path away from, the organisation of production which would fulfil most completely the preferences of consumers.

In fact, of course, there is very little reason to suppose that the authorities of a planned society would resort to pseudo-competition. It is much more probable that they would fall back upon frankly authoritarian planning. They would attempt to manage production as a whole as the general staff manages an army at war.

They would probably retain the price mechanism as an agency for distributing consumers' goods, supplementing it when anything went very wrong by the device of rationing, as in Russia at present. But for the rest they would dictate production from the centre, choosing what kinds and qualities seemed to them most desirable. Such decisions, as we have seen, could not be based on an accounting system with any very precise meaning. The planning authorities would have no way of discovering with any accuracy whether the ends they chose were being secured with an economical use of means. In particular lines of production they could no doubt erect an apparatus which, from the technical point of view, would be very imposing. The Pharaohs did not need a price system for the erection of the pyramids. But at what sacrifice of other goods its products would be secured, at what economic, as distinct from technical, efficiency,[1] it functioned, could not be ascertained. The system would require the complete regimentation of individuals considered as producers. As consumers they could choose between the commodities available. But on the choice of commodities to be produced they would have relatively little influence. They would have to take what it was decided to produce. And what it was decided to produce would be the resultant, not of the conflicting pulls of prices and costs, but of the conflicting advice of different technical experts and politicians with no objective measure to which to submit the multitudinous alternatives possible.

[1] For a more extensive discussion of the difference between the economic and the technical see my *Essay on the Nature and Significance of Economic Science*, chapter ii., also my article on "Production" in the *Encyclopedia of the Social Sciences*, vol. 12. It is perhaps no exaggeration to say that failure to distinguish between the technical and the economic lies at the root of nearly all the major confusions of contemporary economic discussion.

Is it certain that such a system would be more efficient than Capitalism? Is it certain that the friends of liberty and progress who are also friends of planning have sufficiently considered the compatibility of these aims?

8. If the world were united under a single Government, the tendencies of restrictionism which we have already examined would find their logical conclusion in complete world socialism. In the world as we know it, they tend to a world of national socialist economies. If we examine the prospects of a world of this sort, we find further reasons for doubting both its efficiency and its stability.

The authorities of a democratic State which was run on planned lines would presumably postulate, as the object of their plan, the ideal which we have sketched in the previous section—the organisation of production to meet the preferences of consumers. In carrying out the plan, in so far as they were concerned with domestic production, they would encounter the accounting difficulties we have already examined. In so far as they were concerned with production entering into international trade in one way or another, in certain circumstances their task would be facilitated. A socialist State in a non-socialist world enjoys something of the advantages of a municipal undertaking. It can base its calculations on the outside market. It can judge the efficiency of its own enterprise by comparison with costs elsewhere. Because others buy and sell, it can calculate. Of course this is all a matter of degree. A large State doing a small international business with the rest of the world would have small help here in economic calculation. But a small State doing extensive business with the rest of the world might well evade most of the difficulties of economic calculation which would arise under purely socialist conditions.

In such circumstances, the trade policy appropriate to the aim of planning to meet the preferences of individuals would be one which approximated in all important particulars to the traditional free trade policy. The productive resources of the State would be put to the uses for which they were relatively most efficient in price terms. If commodities could be procured more cheaply from abroad, by way of producing something else and sending it in exchange, this would be done. A concern whose costs were higher than the costs of a corresponding concern abroad would cease to receive orders. It would have to go out of business. The capital and labour there employed would have to be put to other uses. The ideal trade policy of a State planned to raise to a maximum the real incomes of its members in all these .formal respects would exactly resemble the trade policy of economic liberalism.

But is there the slightest chance that a State of this kind would in fact pursue such a policy? Can we imagine a socialist State permitting free imports to undercut the products of its own factories? Surely not. All the probabilities point to a policy of restrictionism. Having invested resources in a given set of undertakings, the policy actually adopted would be to maintain their value intact. If this necessitated the exclusion of competing foreign imports, they would be excluded without hesitation. It would be so much easier, it would cause so much less friction with the producers, to do this than to bring about the changes in the organisation of production which the new conditions of international supply and demand made desirable. If the conditions of international trade were such as to call simply for an expansion of established export industries at a constant or rising rate of money incomes, this tendency would not operate. But a planned economy which did not occupy so fortunate a position—an economy whose position in the world was such as to necessitate continual readjustments if the full advantages of international exchange were to be enjoyed—would almost inevitably come to adopt a policy of greater and greater isolation. The ideal socialist policy would be equivalent to the free trade adjustment. The actual policy would be equivalent to something worse than high protectionism.

But all this assumes a planned economy operating within a world of otherwise free enterprise.[1] A world of planned economies would present a totally different picture. It would be a world of geographical syndicalism. Any semblance of a competitive market would have disappeared. Inside the various systems there would be authoritarian disposal of the factors of production; between them a chaos of bilateral bargains between State monopolies. We have seen already the disorder and indeterminateness brought about in Central Europe and elsewhere by the attempt to make barter trade agreements the foundation of trade policy. In a world of planned economies this disorder and indeterminateness would be general.

It is often said that in such circumstances the world of planned States would be merged in a scheme of world planning. We have seen already that there are grave reasons for doubting the efficacy of this particular solution. But, quite apart from this, how improbable is such an outcome. The process which has preceded the

---

[1] This does not exclude the existence of a good deal of petty trade obstruction, tariffs, and so on.

state of affairs we are contemplating is a process which in every direction has strengthened the forces of economic and political nationalism. Vested interests of officialdom and associations of producers, not to mention the emotional forces which tend to be projected upon anything specifically national, would all present barriers to international union much more formidable than any yet existing. A world in which the movement of goods, of money and of people, is restrained and impeded by national organisation is a world in which the achievement of the international ideal, whether on Socialist or Liberal lines, is more distant even than it is at present. It is mere self-deception to believe, as so many Socialists now believe, that such developments are an "inevitable stage" in the "right line" of evolution, just as it is self-deception to urge that it is right to arm further to facilitate disarmament, to erect tariffs in order to promote free trade, and so on. These are not cases of *reculer pour mieux sauter*; they are cases of recoiling to jump in the opposite direction. Nationalism and internationalism in the field of economic organisation are inimical to each other. Whatever leads to the one must inevitably lead from the other.

It is difficult to believe that in such a world international peace would be safer, or national productivity higher, than in a world of free enterprise. International division of labour would be less; international investments almost negligible. To the existing causes of political friction between States would be added a host of economic frictions which do not arise when international trading is in private hands. A world of national planning is not a world which offers high hopes of political stability or economic progress.

CHAPTER VIII

CONDITIONS OF RECOVERY

1. UNDER what conditions might we hope for stable recovery? It is not the function of the economist to frame a day-to-day programme of action. But if his diagnosis is correct, it should enable him to describe the general conditions which must be satisfied if the disorders he has indicated are to disappear. Whether it is ultimately desirable that they should disappear it is not within his capacity as economist to judge. On the basis of what has been said in earlier chapters, therefore, an attempt will now be made to outline the conditions under which business might be expected to revive and the tendencies to extreme instability, so characteristic of the post-war period, might in some degree be eliminated. Complete stability is probably unattainable. But experience suggests that there are causes of instability which could be eliminated if it were so desired.

2. The first essential of any recovery from the position in which the world now finds itself is a return of business confidence. Much as has been done in various ways to eliminate the causes of the initial dislocations, men will not recommence business operations, they will not undertake new commitments of any but the most transitory nature, unless they have confidence in the future. The revival of industry in the lines where

it is most depressed—in the capital-producing industries—depends upon a revival of willingness to take
long-term risks, to plan for a future beyond the day
after to-morrow. Enterprise is the assumption of risk.
But when risk is too great enterprise will not be undertaken.

But how is confidence to be restored?

It should be quite clear from what has been said
already, that, political complications apart, the main
danger to confidence at the present time is the fear of
monetary disturbance. A world in which the exchanges
fluctuate on the scale on which they have fluctuated
during the last three years is not a place in which
any general revival of business can be expected. Local
revivals there may be, in the areas benefited by relative
under-valuation. But world-wide revival cannot come
from such causes. While this very paragraph was being
written, there came news of the depreciation of yet
another currency. Before it is printed, there may be
many more. There can be no healthy recovery on such
a basis. So long as there is danger either of loss of
markets through exchange fluctuations, or loss of
capital through internal inflation, investment will hang
fire and revival be retarded. The first essential of
world-wide recovery is some degree of stabilisation of
the foreign exchanges.

It is often said that stabilisation of this sort should
not be attempted until prices have risen. Until prices
have risen to the level at which they stood before the
slump started, it is urged, it is wrong to think about
exchange stabilisation. When we are back at the 1926
price-level, and not before, it will be time to discuss
such refinements as exchange stability. Such has been
the view of the English reflationists. Such was the

ground on which President Roosevelt destroyed the prospects of the World Economic Conference.

Now it may be freely admitted that the level of prices, which exists at the bottom of a great depression, is not a level which it is desirable to perpetuate. No one who has followed the analysis of the earlier chapters of this book will be disposed to question the existence of deflationary tendencies which have reduced the general level of prices considerably below the level which the purely technical tendencies operative before the slump began would have led one to expect. No one will deny that the presence of unusual risks in the shape of exchange fluctuations, apprehensions of political disturbances and the like, has held up spending to a degree which has been highly deflationary. It is quite clear that if confidence were restored there would be such an increase of spending as would raise certain prices considerably.

But it is one thing for prices to rise as a result of the restoration of confidence. It is quite another to attempt to push them up by deliberate monetary manipulation. A rise in prices which comes from a return of confidence is a movement which may be viewed without apprehension, provided that it is not too quick and that it does not go too far. (The sudden uprush which comes from relief from undue panic, as in the United States in the May and June of 1933, is not of this order.) But the rise of prices which comes from the anticipation of inflation, the upward spurt which comes from a momentary gain in the race of competitive depreciation, these are movements which, so far from creating the basis of lasting confidence, are likely to destroy the basis in which lasting confidence can be built. Two years ago, when the present writer and others drew

attention to the real danger of competitive depreciation to which the policy of isolated reflation was leading, fears of this sort were treated as academic and
illusory. At the present day, if they are to be discredited, they must be described by other adjectives.[1]
Failure to stabilise at an earlier date on the part of
Great Britain was one of the main causes of the abandonment of the Gold Standard by the United States
of America. Failure to stabilise generally at the World
Economic Conference was one of the main causes of
the present grave economic and political difficulties
of the different members of the Gold Block, among
which are to be counted the most conspicuous of the
remaining parliamentary democracies of continental
Europe. If democracy goes by the board altogether,
among the chief States of continental Europe, the
chaos of international exchanges since 1931, although
by no means the only cause, will have played a not
unimportant rôle in bringing about the disaster.

As for the view that what is necessary is to raise
prices to the 1929 or to the 1926 level, it is perhaps unnecessary to waste much time in argument. Whatever
may have been its influence two years ago—and as we
have seen it was the main cause for the British refusal
to co-operate in repairing the ravages of the disaster
of 1931—at the present day it is coming to be realised
that as an objective it is not merely illusory, but
positively harmful. If the analysis which has been developed in these pages is correct, one of the main
causes of the present difficulties was the inflationary
boom of 1927-29. To raise prices from their present
level to the level of the pre-slump period would be to
run the risk of a repetition of this disaster. Already it is

---

[1] See a correspondence in the pages of the *Economist*, May 1932.

abundantly clear that if recovery gets going at all—and of course it is not certain that it will not be frustrated by war or by Government policy—one of the main tasks of the monetary authorities will be to prevent it flaring up into a wild boom whose collapse might well be associated with consequences even more disastrous than anything which has happened in the present depression. The policies which have been pursued by the Central Banks in the attempt to counter deflation have resulted in the creation of a basis for credit expansion much more considerable than that existing at the commencement of the slump.[1] If business prospects were to brighten and confidence were to be restored, it would probably be incumbent on the authorities actually to contract this basis if things were not to get out of hand. To carry through such a policy of business stabilisation and at the same time to attempt to get back to the price-level of 1926 are not compatible undertakings.

3. It is clear, then, that some kind of provisional stabilisation of exchanges is the first condition of permanent recovery. Having regard to the incredible confusion into which the world has been thrown by the exchange policy of the United States, it is improbable that anything more than provisional stabilisation can be hoped for until sufficient time has elapsed for it to be seen whether the new parities are appropriate to the permanent elements in the situation. It would certainly be most unwise to attempt to restore the Gold Standard under conditions which would make its operation impossible. The countries which are now off the Gold Standard will do well to follow the example

[1] See Chart above, Chapter II. p. 18, and Tables 13 and 14, Statistical Appendix.

set by the French in 1927 rather than that set by the British in 1925, in bringing about a final stabilisation of the exchanges.

But while provisional stabilisation must come first, final stabilisation must come later, if full recovery on a world-wide scale is to be possible. There can be no revival of international lending, no extensive reduction of obstacles to international trade, until uncertainty with regard to the exchanges is finally at an end. Until international investment revives, until international trade is relieved of some, at least, of the impediments which now hinder its operation, it is futile to hope for recovery to reach a very high level. This consideration is important for all countries dependent to any great extent upon relations with the outside world, but it is especially germane to the circumstances of Great Britain. Important as are the new industries catering for the home market, there can be no full restoration of prosperity for this country, without a considerable restoration of international trade and international investment.

On what basis should such stabilisation take place? It is clear that two things are desirable. Firstly, that monetary conditions in different parts of the world should be kept in a relationship conducive to international equilibrium—that the local movements of money and credit should be such as to bring about those movements of relative prices necessary to avoid a breakdown of the régime of stabilised exchanges. Secondly, that monetary conditions in the world as a whole should be such as to avoid the creation of large fluctuations of trade and industry by the generation of inflationary booms. Let us examine these requirements separately.

So far as the preservation of interlocal equilibrium is concerned, it is clear that the main requirement is a mechanism which allows payments between individuals and groups of individuals living in different countries to exercise the same effect on prices as would be exercised by similar payments between individuals and groups of individuals living in the same country—a mechanism which puts payments between *countries* on the same footing as payments between *counties*. If, on balance, the payments made from Edinburgh to London in a certain period exceed the payments made from London to Edinburgh, it is necessary, if equilibrium is to be preserved, that there should be a contraction of balances in Edinburgh and an expansion in London. If this does not happen—if balances in London are increased and balances in Edinburgh are not diminished—then there is a net inflation, and the disequilibrium in the trade balance will continue. Precisely the same thing is true of international payments. The requirement of equilibrium is that the movements of active balances should exactly balance each other. If this does not take place, if in one centre there is "offsetting" in the sense of creating new credit to take the place of the credit which has been transferred, then the conditions of equilibrium are not satisfied. As we have already seen, under conditions of this sort, most disastrous inflations may be generated.

It is clear that such requirements would be fulfilled by a banking system which was completely unified and international. The balances in the various branches in different parts of the world would expand and contract automatically with the payments in and out of the various customers. It would be within the power of the controlling authority to maintain effective international and interlocal equilibrium.

Such a system is not practicable. In a world of separate States, it is highly improbable that complete surrender of the right to regulate the conditions of supply of money would be made by the various nations. It is an open question, on quite other grounds, whether such a complete elimination of separate banks is desirable. In any case we may be quite sure that such an arrangement is not immediately probable. International equilibrium will not be secured on these lines.

But the advantages of such an arrangement can be secured in a much more practical manner. If the various Central Banks agree to buy and sell one of the precious metals at a fixed price and if they regulate the volume of credit in their respective areas by reference to the fluctuations in their holdings of these metals, expanding as they increase, contracting as they contract, and rigorously avoiding "offsetting" credit creation, the same effects will be secured as regards interlocal adjustment as if the money of all these countries were exclusively composed of the precious metal or if the credit arrangements of the world were in the hands of one bank. If prices and costs in a particular area are too high in relation to the world conditions of supply and demand, payments out will exceed payments in. Elsewhere the reverse state of affairs will prevail. Payments out will tend to be made by shipments of the precious metal which forms the common basis of the different countries. If no "offsetting" takes place, there will be a tendency for prices and costs in the different areas to be brought into equilibrium.

But what is this but that most maligned and misunderstood institution, the Gold Standard, run, not on the inflationist lines which caused its breakdown in the years after the war, but on the strict lines which the theory of the Gold Standard rightly understood has always postulated? It was the *rationale* of the Gold Standard in the sense in which it was always understood by its intelligent supporters—it is not really very clever to pretend that the bulk of expert opinion in the past has always been actuated by ignorant prejudice—that it imposed on a world of separate national States and national currencies the same conditions as would obtain if the currency system were truly international. To be on the Gold Standard in this sense meant that although the various national monies might have different units of account yet the value or these units was kept in a fixed relationship. International payments had the same significance as inter-county payments. Arbitrary increases in the local supply of money could take place only at the risk of being forced off the Gold Standard.

It is quite clear that such a system is not fool-proof. It is not "automatic" in the sense that it is independent of human volition. As we have seen since the war, if it is attempted to work it without regard for the rules which constitute its *raison d'être*, it breaks down. But so far as international adjustments are concerned it sets a clear objective of policy. It possesses powerful psychological sanctions. It provides a basis on which men can trade and invest internationally with some degree of confidence. The pre-war world in which such a system prevailed was not immune from general cyclical fluctuations but, save in outlying parts, it was reasonably immune from the evils of fluctuating exchanges and the paralysis of capital movements.

This it owed to the Gold Standard. The achievement of even such a limited degree of stability would seem to be a worthy object of policy in our own time.

But what about our second requirement, a monetary system which avoids the generation of general fluctuations?

It is quite clear that there is nothing in the Gold Standard as such which precludes the generation of such fluctuations. It is possible to conceive them arising under a monetary system consisting solely of gold coins and token money with no bank credit. Once bank credit is taken into account, the probability of their occurrence, in the absence of policy directed to secure their elimination, becomes much greater. It is clear that the accidental variations of geological discovery and mining technique do not necessarily guarantee fluctuations of money supply conducive to the elimination of cyclical fluctuations. Discovery of this truism has often afforded great satisfaction to first-year students and platform speakers in search of cheap effects.

But this is by no means decisive against the Gold Standard. It is clear that it is a safeguard against gross inflation. Uncontrolled, it permits a certain degree of inflation which no doubt may be very damaging. But it sets a limit to such movements which does not exist under a free standard. It is unfortunately true that in the past there is no example of a paper standard which has not sooner or later suffered a degree of depreciation inconceivable under any probable condition of the Gold Standard. Moreover, if run according to the rules inherent in the logic of its conception it is a safeguard against local depreciation. There can be little doubt that the extreme severity of the present depression is due in part to the fact that it was the result of an inflation conditioned by local disequilibrium. As we have seen, the American inflation would never have gone so far had it not been for the disequilibrium of Great Britain. The American inflation is a product of the absence of a banking policy on Gold Standard lines.

Beyond this—and for those who have hopes that in time the growth of knowledge will permit the smoothing out of the worst excesses of cyclical fluctuation, this is the important consideration—there is nothing in the Gold Standard as such which precludes concerted action for the stabilisation of business on the part of the Central Banks concerned. Examination of the probable trend of the gold supply during the next two decades does not suggest any mechanical obstacle to a policy of this kind. A "shortage" of gold in the sense of an absolute diminution or a failure of supply to increase as rapidly as the gold-using population is improbable. A rapid increase—itself conducive to large inflation on a world scale—is also unlikely. With prices at anything near their present level the present supply should be ample to permit of adequate reserves for such Central Banks as want them. For the rest, the possibility of concerted variation of reserve requirements by Central Banks should be quite sufficient to ensure that the fact that their respective systems were linked to gold should not be an obstacle to the carrying out of prudent action designed to mitigate the instability of business.

But what form should that action take? It would be lacking in candour to suggest that at the present time we are in a position to draw up any very precise set of rules for such action. Our knowledge of the more intricate mechanism of fluctuations is far from complete, and it is with the more intricate mechanism that a Central Bank policy which is not to be intolerably wooden and clumsy must be concerned. There is not complete agreement among economists upon these matters. It is agreed that to prevent the depression the only effective method is to prevent the boom. But how this is to be done is not a matter on which there exists unanimity. Certain economists, impressed by the analysis whereby it is established that the policy of the stable price-level is not necessarily conducive to general stability, now urge that the object of policy should be the stabilisation of incomes—that is, a price-level falling with increased productivity. With the general theoretical background of this proposal it is possible to feel considerable sympathy. Many of the propositions in this essay are based upon similar analysis. But at the same time it is still possible to feel considerable scepticism concerning the adequacy of such a prescription. The price-level is a crude index for the carrying out of so intricate a policy as the smoothing out of the trade cycle. It is insensitive and slow to respond to what may well be important changes of tendency. A policy which waits on movements of the price-level before taking the action necessary to arrest the development of a boom may well miss the main opportunity of carrying out its intentions. Much more promising, and at the same time much more practical—at least in the opinion of the present writer—is the suggestion that the banks should pay chief attention to the movements of the security markets and that group of prices which is especially sensitive to movements of interest rates. If, as soon as there appeared signs of a general boom on security markets, the Central Banks were to take action to bring it to an end, it seems probable that extremes of business fluctuations might be avoided. Certainly this is a policy which would have averted much of the distresses from which the world has been suffering recently.

But whatever may be the truth in this very difficult matter, one thing seems tolerably certain. The policy of stabilising the general level of prices and ignoring all other movements is a snare and a delusion. It was this policy, conjoined with that other policy of frustrating the effects of gold movements, to which we have already alluded, which was largely responsible for the catastrophe of 1929. Again and again during the boom years we were assured by men who should have known better that the trade cycle had been eliminated, that so long as prices did not rise there was no fear of over-expansion, that the boom in land and common stocks was merely a reflection of the increased value of property, and that if there were any sign of a fall of prices due to a transfer of expenditure to Stock Exchange and real-estate speculation, then the Central Banks should create more credit to support the speculation. This policy was pursued. Yet such is the inflexibility of the human mind that, in spite of all that it led to, there are yet to be heard voices urging that a similar policy should be adopted in the next period of prosperity. It is no accident that they are the voices of men who failed utterly to see what was happening before the depression, and who throughout the slump, no doubt with the best will in the world, have consistently supported those policies which have arrested liquidation, prolonged uncertainty and delayed the coming of recovery.

4. It is the argument of the preceding section that a condition of final recovery is the restoration of an international Gold Standard managed with a view to

preserving interlocal equilibrium and avoiding the development of booms. There can be little doubt that at the present time a policy of this sort commands the approval of a growing body of expert opinion. But it is by no means generally accepted. In this country, at any rate, there are those who favour a more separatist policy. They are willing to undertake a provisional stabilisation. They are willing to preserve a certain relation between the national currency and gold. But they are unwilling to fix a permanent parity. A Gold Standard with movable parities, not merely during the period of provisional stabilisation but also as a permanent arrangement, is the object of their policy. Such influences must not be under-estimated. It is necessary, therefore, to give full consideration to their case. Incidentally this will cast further light on the position here adopted.[1]

The case for a Gold Standard with movable parities is essentially the case for an independent national standard. The arguments by which it is supported are essentially the arguments by which the case for independent paper standards has been supported in the past. It should be clear that a system under which interlocal adjustments are carried out, not by the gold-flow mechanism with its local expansions and contractions of credit, but by alterations of the par of exchange, is no Gold Standard at all in the strict sense of the word. In its working it resembles the paper system of pure theory. But because paper does not inspire confidence, because the constant fluctuations of paper are obviously damaging, it works behind a gold façade.

The arguments for such a system are twofold. On

---

[1] The argument of this section is necessarily somewhat technical; the next section takes up the thread of the general argument of the chapter.

the one hand it is hoped that in this way it will be possible to insulate, as it were, the area in which it prevails from the general fluctuations of business which occur in the outside world. On the other hand it is claimed that it provides a more effective method of adaptation to changes in world conditions. Under the Gold Standard proper, a change in the conditions of world supply and demand may involve a contraction of credit and a lowering of prices and incomes. Under the Gold Standard with movable parities, a change in the par of exchange will be sufficient.

The two arguments are not equally persuasive. The claim that a national system will be enabled to insulate the area in which it prevails from general fluctuations of business is not at all convincing. We can leave undiscussed the desirability of a mechanism which permits experiments in local inflation. (The possibility of varying the exchange removes the check of the gold flow). History affords no ground for confidence that such experiments will not be attempted, and, as we have seen, there is not yet sufficient agreement on the policy of monetary management to justify any very great confidence in supposing that one area will do better in this respect than the combined efforts of the banks of the world as a whole. But, even if we ignore these grave practical difficulties, there still remains the important general question, Can a system, which is in communication with the rest of the world, insulate itself from world fluctuations by a device of this nature? General reasoning affords no presumption that it can. Indeed if the analysis of earlier chapters be correct, there is a certain presumption that it cannot. For if it be true that a business cycle is generated by movements of interest rates which affect *relative* prices in such a way as to cause false expectation, there is no reason to suppose that a policy of local management directed to keeping the local price-level constant or gently falling would prevent the transmission of such changes arising in other parts of the world. If prices *in general* in one part of the world moved differently from prices in the managed area, there would pre sumably be a shift in exchange rates. But this shift in exchange rates would not itself affect the relative profitability of different stages of production. If prices in the capital-producing industries in the rest of the world were affording a greater profit margin, then the fact that the British exchange rate moved against the rest of the world would not prevent the British capital-producing industries receiving also a relative stimulus. It is not at all clear that the fluctuating exchange by itself is an effective insulator against this kind of fluctuation. The principles of monetary management which, in such circumstances, would eliminate disturbance have yet to be enunciated.

The argument for independence and insulation, therefore, is much less persuasive than might at first be imagined. The argument for automatic adjustment to changes in the terms of trade, however, is on a much less fragile footing. It is quite clear that the rigidity of costs in certain areas has been one of the great obstacles to the successful functioning of an international standard. It is clear that in the future it may give rise to difficulties. A system which eliminated such difficulties without countervailing disadvantages would have much to recommend it. The question is, does it? Are there no countervailing disadvantages? It is this question which is fundamental to the correct judgement of this proposal.

It is important to realise the exact object of the
system if we are not to attach undue weight to the
result which it promises. If the fundamental conditions
of international trade bring about a lowering of the
equilibrium real terms of trade, then no power in the
world can prevent real incomes from being lowered or
unemployment from being created. If the demand for
Australian wool falls off, nothing can prevent the real
receipts derived from the sale of wool from being
lowered. The sole purpose of the device of the fluctuating exchange, therefore, is to put the receivers of fixed
money-incomes (contract wages, etc.) into the same
position as those who sell directly in the world market.
It is as though the people in the area concerned were
to say: "We know that the goods we sell in the world
market fetch a smaller weight of gold, but we don't
like admitting that the weight is smaller. We will
therefore change the unit of weight and pretend our
incomes are the same." Only of course they *don't* know
it. The essence of the device is to carry through the
adjustment without causing trouble. How long it would
be before wage-earners and others began to think in
terms of real instead of money wages, and whether it
would not be simpler in the end to instruct them in the
elementary theory of markets, we may leave undiscussed for the moment. Our question is rather, are there
accompanying disadvantages?

There can be no doubt that such a system would
impose considerable limitations on international investment. Long-term contracts between the inhabitants
of the different national areas would be subject to the
risk of an alteration in the relative gold content of the
respective currencies. A world of Gold Standards with
movable parities would be a world in which the volume

of international investment would be considerably reduced.

Is this effect undesirable? A few years ago there would have been almost unanimous agreement that it was. The benefits of putting free resources to the point of maximum return were so obvious; the part played by the movement of international capital in the development of the modern world was so conspicuous. Who could have argued that the time had come to call a halt to such a process—that what had made possible the enormous increase in wealth of the last hundred years had now ceased to have any function? And at the present day, if we survey the wreckage left behind by the slump, the crushing shortage of capital in those parts of the world least able to provide it, can it seriously be argued that a revival of international lending would be anything but beneficial? Nevertheless, there can be no doubt that there has been a certain change of opinion. The slump has brought disillusionment. So many of the international investments made in the pre-slump period have proved to have been misplaced, so much money that was sent abroad in those days has been irretrievably lost, that to say that a certain measure will diminish the volume of international lending does not nowadays arouse the apprehension that it would have done in the days before the slump.

This attitude is surely unreasonable. Unquestionably in the past there have been grave mistakes in the business of international lending. Unquestionably in the future there will exist political risks which will militate against a revival of international investment. It is certainly desirable that greater prudence should be exercised in the flotation of foreign loans. But the fact that risks which were previously ignored are now recognised and that risks which did not before exist have now come into being is no argument for an arrangement which introduces yet another limitation on business. The fluctuating exchange discriminates equally against all foreign loans of the same class, whether good or bad. It does not really seem a sensible plan to deal with one set of risks by calling another into existence.

Beyond this—and this is a consideration which has especial importance for Great Britain—it is important not to underestimate the structural and monetary implications of a great diminution of the volume of international lending. The structure of industry all over the world has been based on the expectation of large volumes of international capital transfer. The export industries of countries like Great Britain depend even in their present shape upon a substantial volume of capital export. If this is to cease, these industries will have to be abandoned or totally transformed. Moreover, the monetary effects of such a curtailment are not such as to warrant the expectation of a smooth transition. If the custom of exporting capital from the centres in which the rate of return on investment is relatively low to centres where it is relatively high is to cease, the long-term equilibrium rate in the erstwhile capital-exporting centres must be very much lower than accords with present expectations. This means a danger that long-term investment will hang fire, that balances will accumulate and, in short, that that persistence of deflationary tendencies in the system, which we all deplore, may be indefinitely prolonged.

But this is not all. Quite apart from its effect on

long-term investment, the existence of a Gold Standard with movable parities is likely to create a highly dangerous and deflationary situation in the short-term market. We have seen already, in an earlier chapter, how the existence of abnormally large funds of liquid resources, ready to migrate at short notice from one centre to another, has caused dislocation and difficulty in the chief money markets of the world. The setting up as a final arrangement of a Gold Standard with movable parities is likely to cause such a state of affairs to be permanent. The prospect of alterations of parity creates opportunities of investment which definitely provoke extraordinary transfers of capital. There have been abundant examples in the last few years. So soon as it is thought that the parity may be altered there develops an abnormal situation in the forward market. Short-term funds begin to distribute themselves in a wholly abnormal manner—flying from the centre where downward valuation is expected, piling up in the centres where consequential appreciation is likely. It is difficult to see how this can be avoided. What dealer operating in short money, who has reason to anticipate a downward valuation of the money of the centre in which he is operating, will not regard this as a suitable occasion for an in-and-out operation? It is pretty clear that a régime of this sort must necessitate the most extensive measures of exchange control and probably the nationalisation of the entire apparatus of the capital market. Some may find this unobjectionable; if so, they should say so explicitly.

Such difficulties would accompany a régime in which the parities were moved only in accordance with the "ideal" theoretical requirements. In practice it is improbable that the movements would be of this order.

The advocates of this scheme often speak as if the ascertainment of the appropriate movements of the parities would be a simple matter. In fact it would be a matter of the utmost difficulty. In works on theory, in which the movements of exchanges are discussed, it is assumed that the movements of the real terms of trade, etc., which occasion such movements, are given. In practice they would have to be discovered, and this is no easy matter. To gauge the equilibrium exchange rate it is not enough to know how technical productivity in different areas is developing, though this is sufficiently difficult. It is necessary to know the movements in relative demand for different kinds of goods, to gauge the effects of the import and export of capital. It is impossible to believe that the authorities would hit the nail on the head nearly so often as they would if they were simply trying to maintain the Gold Standard. And if they did not hit the nail on the head there would arise all those tendencies to international disequilibrium which, since the over-valuation of the pound and the under-valuation of the franc, we have learned to know so well.

All this, moreover, assumes that the question of the parity could be kept out of politics. But is it not almost certain that it could not? No doubt there is no guarantee that the working of the Gold Standard itself may not be the subject of political debate and influence. This sometimes happens. But can there be any doubt that if the alteration of gold parities were to come to be regarded—to use the terms of one of its supporters— as "the most natural and easy means of adjusting the international position of countries *vis-à-vis* one another", it would become one of the most natural and easy ways of appealing to the electorate? Can the supporters of this policy contemplate with equanimity the disturbance in the sphere of industry and finance in a world in which mob voting on the parity was one of the staple items of democratic elections? Would it not be one of the most certain methods of discrediting democracy?

But even if such a matter could be kept out of domestic politics, is it probable that it would not create injurious repercussions in international relationships? This of course is a matter of practical judgement, not of analytical economics. But it seems fairly clear that competitive depreciation, the erection of anti-exchange-dumping duties, systems of discriminating licensing and the like, would be the almost inevitable accompaniment of any manipulation of exchange rates. It would be all very well for the supporters of such manipulations to go round to the politicians of the nations undertaking such reprisals, and to say: "My dear friends, your apprehensions are groundless; we are only altering the exchange to correspond with the alteration of the real terms of trade. You must realise that this is in the interests of international equilibrium." This is not the sort of story which will go down with the manufacturers of competing exports. No doubt Gold Standard adjustments, too, may have the effect of intensifying international competition, and may occasionally provoke tariff reprisals. It is improbable that they would lead to the kind of competition in depreciation and trade restriction which seems the most likely outcome of alterations of parity. There will be no substantial reduction of tariffs in a world of movable parities.

What, then, are we to say of the device of movable parities? It follows from what has been said already that the disturbance and limitations upon the smooth

working of the economic machinery which it brings
into being are in all probability even greater than the
disturbances and difficulties which we know may accompany the working of the Gold Standard. It follows,
too, that these disturbances and difficulties are almost
inseparable from the device as such, whereas the disturbances and difficulties which have accompanied the
working of the Gold Standard are not bound up with
the Gold Standard itself but spring from causes which
with greater knowledge and goodwill we might hope to
see dissipated. But in matters of this sort we must not
abstract too much. It is improbable that in the next
few years all the outlying raw material producing
centres will restore the Gold Standard. And so far as
the smaller areas, which in the past have probably
already borrowed too much, are concerned, it is conceivable that the disadvantages of such an arrangement may not be too great, nor the repercussions on
world stability very considerable. But so far as the
great financial centres of the world—London, Paris,
New York, Amsterdam—are concerned, the weight of
argument is all the other way. If these centres do not
establish a common monetary system which permits
confidence in the future and eliminates uncertainty
with regard to the exchanges, the continuance of the
process of recovery to a very high level is improbable,
and the danger of a relapse into severe financial crisis
is very grave.

5. A stabilisation of exchanges and an eventual
restoration of an international monetary system, run
on the lines indicated above, would probably afford the
basis for a considerable recovery of business if political
conditions were favourable—if there were no war and
if domestic policy in the various countries was not such

as seriously to disturb confidence. Over a wide spread of business activity, in one way or another, there has probably been sufficient liquidation and cost reduction to restore the prospects of profit if monetary instability is eliminated. But recovery cannot be general, nor can it be expected to reach a very high level, so long as the various barriers and impediments to international trade which have grown up in the post-war period, especially since the slump, remain at their present high level. Full recovery, let alone future progress, depends upon the removal of, at any rate, the worst of these obstacles.

It is important that in considering this matter we should preserve a sense of proportion. As has been argued in an earlier section, the existence of protective tariffs on a considerable scale is not in itself an obstacle to extensive business activity nor to a fairly rapid rate of progress. During the period before the war there existed extensive systems of protective tariffs, and although there can be little doubt that they were inimical to the full exploitation of the advantages of the division of labour, they did not prevent that considerable advance of wealth per head which was characteristic of that period. No one in his senses would argue that the establishment of universal free trade is a *sine qua non* of business recovery at the present. But the obstacles which limit international business at the present time are on so much more extensive a scale than in the pre-war period, and are of a kind so much more disturbing to trade, that the situation created by their existence differs not only in degree but in kind from the situation of those days. In central Europe at the present time, to be called a Free Trader it is not necessary to cease to support a régime of high protection; it is

necessary only to oppose the existing systems of import
licences, exchange controls and quota restrictions. Before the world can hope for general recovery, these
obstacles at least must be swept away. In the present
situation a moderate tariff is a relatively minor evil. A
return even to the pre-slump level of tariffs would be a
most powerful stimulus to recovery.

This is not to say that there is anything to be said
for tariffs as a positive means to prosperity. Nothing
that has been said in recent years has served to alter
in any substantial respect the strength of the case for
the maximum international division of labour, that is
the case against protective tariffs; and the technical
developments of modern industry have done much to
make that case even more pertinent than in the past.
The economies of mass production, which modern
technical developments make possible, are economies
which can only be reaped to the full if the market is
sufficiently extensive. Since tariffs necessarily contract markets, it follows that the existence of tariffs
must prevent resort to the economies of mass production being as widespread as might otherwise be the
case. A world of national States each striving for
economic autarchy is a world in which the economies
of large-scale production can never be fully exploited.
A removal of the grosser obstacles to trade would be
a powerful stimulus to recovery. But the world would
continue to be poorer than it need be if it were content with tariffs at the pre-slump level. The creation
of an economic machinery more immune from fluctuations, and capable of making available for mankind
the full fruits of technical progress, must involve a
definite reversal of the trade policies which have imposed increasing limitation on world trade since the

seventies, and a return to the policy of a progressive freeing of trade.

6. A removal of the grosser obstacles to trade and the prospect of a lowering of tariff barriers would do much to enhance a recovery made possible by a stabilisation of monetary conditions. Neither monetary policy nor the freeing of trade can guarantee a lasting stability of business conditions, if the underlying structure of business costs and organisation does not regain its capacity for adaptation to change. As has been emphasised in an earlier chapter, we misread altogether the lesson of the present depression if we attribute its violence solely to monetary disturbances. As we have seen, the nature of the structure within which these monetary disturbances took place, the failure of Great Britain to get into international equilibrium, the delay in liquidation and cost reduction all over the world in 1930, not to mention the instability of State-aided monopolies and pools, also played a large part. It is quite certain that if, in the future, the price system becomes more rigid and business structure more inflexible, then the danger that oscillations which otherwise might be of quite a minor order may develop into fluctuations of the same or even greater order of magnitude will be very greatly enhanced. Price rigidity and an ossified business structure would only be supportable in a period in which the tempo of change was very slow. But the tempo of change in our times is very rapid.

In recent years, the consequences of inflexibility have been particularly apparent in the labour market. As we have seen already, it would be a mistake to say that the existence of a large body of unemployment is necessarily due in the first instance to wage rates which have been pushed above the point at which employment would be normal. The initial change may come as a result of some monetary maladjustment—the restoration of the exchange at too high a level for instance; or it may originate in some movement of the conditions of real demand for the products of the industry or industries in question. Nor is it true to argue that if wage rates were perfectly plastic all unemployment would disappear. Some unemployment exists at the height of prosperity, and in times of severe slump a complete absorption of all the unemployed within a very short period is not to be hoped for. But in general it is true to say that a greater flexibility of wage rates would considerably reduce unemployment; in particular, that a greater flexibility of wage rates in the industries first affected by fluctuations would almost certainly diminish the spread and the violence of the repercussions of these movements. If it had not been for the prevalence of the view that wage rates must at all costs be maintained in order to maintain the purchasing power of the consumer, the violence of the present depression and the magnitude of the unemployment which has accompanied it would have been considerably less. If the obstacles to cost adjustment in Great Britain had been less formidable the whole history of the last ten years would have been different.

This is a hard saying, and there can be little wonder that men of humanity, especially those who are not themselves of the wage-earning classes and who therefore feel a natural reluctance to say anything which may seem to imply a desire that the position of others should be even temporarily worsened, should be loath to accept it. But it can be rejected only as a result of failure to perceive the significance of the wage contract in the organisation of modern industry. If industry were run by groups of independent producers and if the demand for their products were to fall off, it would be inevitable either that prices would have to be lowered or that some of the products would remain unsold. If the buyers in the market place a lower valuation on the product but the sellers maintain their prices, then they are left with supplies on their hands. But substantially the same is true when industry is organised by capitalist employers. The employers sell the products of industry and pay the wage-earners out of the capital thus maintained. If there is a diminution of demand, the first impact of the shock falls upon profits. It is right that this should be so, for it is the function of the *entrepreneur* to assume the main risks of enterprise. But profits are not indefinitely squeezable, nor are the other non-wage elements in costs. So that if the fluctuation is at all severe, either there must be some downward modification of wage rates or some of the labour offered at the old price must remain unemployed. This conclusion is abundantly borne out by experience. Unemployment is predominantly a phenomenon of those industries where the market for labour and the market for the product are separated, as it were, by the wage contract. The areas of unemployment to-day are the areas of contract wages. Peasant producers are not unemployed in trade fluctuations. They suffer an automatic reduction of money-income.

Once this is clear, the attitude of the true humanitarian must surely assume a new complexion. He will naturally be anxious that the wage-earner should receive the full value of his part in the production of the product. But he will realise too that a policy which holds wage rates rigid when the equilibrium rate has altered, is a policy which creates unemployment. He will regard it as hypocritical to blame the policy of the trade unions more than, or even as much as, he would blame other attempts at monopolistic restriction. But he will remember too the victim of monopolistic restriction, the unemployed man who is prevented by the policy of maintaining wage rates from disposing of his labour at a price at which it is possible for the consumer to be induced to purchase the product. And he will regard with some contempt the attitude of those who, unwilling to face the facts of poverty, content themselves with approving the enforcement of a wage higher than industry can bear and avert their gaze from the unemployment which they have thus created, or deceive themselves that it springs from other causes.

It is sometimes said that this proposition that unemployment could be diminished and fluctuations avoided by a greater plasticity of wage rates involves the view that wages should be reduced indefinitely and trade unions prohibited by law. Such assertions rest either upon crass ignorance or deliberate misrepresentation. With a free demand for labour there is no probability of an indefinite reduction of wage rates. Nor is the disappearance of trade unions a necessary feature of the restoration of flexibility of wage rates. As selling and negotiating agents, trade unions perform a function which, if guided by a right conception of policy, may well be conducive to the smooth functioning of the market for labour. They prevent petty exploitation and they eliminate a multiplicity of individual bargains. What is necessary is that their policy shall be guided by considerations of employment, and that they shall not be allowed to prevent from working those who, in order to avoid unemployment, are prepared to accept a rate lower than the rate which has previously prevailed. In order that the market should be reasonably free it is not at all necessary that trade unions should be prohibited. It is necessary only that they, equally with other would-be monopolists, should receive no support from the Government, either direct or indirect.

7. But this brings us back to our main contention, the necessity for the elimination of all kinds of inflexibility. In order that recovery may be assured and future dislocations minimised, it is necessary not only that flexibility should be restored to the prices of different kinds of labour but that flexibility should also be restored in other markets. There is strong reason for attributing much of the severity of the depression to the inflexibility of cartel prices and to the insecurity caused by the existence of giant buying agencies in the various commodity markets. If future fluctuations are to be avoided it is necessary that these things should disappear.

But how is this to be done? The answer is not very difficult. As we have seen already, the worst cases of market rigidity, or of insecurity of industrial structure, are the creation of Government policy. Cartel prices have never shown themselves unduly inflexible when the cartels could not depend upon a tariff or other forms of State support. Industrial monopoly, where it does not depend upon natural monopoly, is usually the by-product of Protection or a system of trade marks and patent legislation definitely inimical to competition. Pools and restriction schemes flourish chiefly when they receive Government support. It would be

foolish to pretend that the structure of capitalistic industry is such as continually to achieve the ideal competitive adjustment. But it is fairly clear that the most
conspicuous failures to tend in this direction depend in
one way or another on authoritarian measures which
tend to foster monopoly.

If, therefore, it is desired to eliminate these sources
of instability, the policies of States in relation to industry must undergo complete revision. It must be a
maxim of State policy to do nothing to bolster up
monopoly. The habit of intervening to prop up unsound positions and to support particular interests
must cease. Nothing must be done which will encourage
business men to believe that they will not be allowed
to go under if they make mistakes or if the conditions
of the market make necessary a contraction of their
industry. Instead of being more and more an official
of the State, hampered on all sides by administrative
rules and regulations, the business man should be freed
as far as possible to perform that function which is his
main justification in a society organised, not for the
benefit of the part but of the whole, namely, the assumption of risk and the planning of initiative. The
same principle must underlie the treatment of private
property. Property must be left to stand on its own
legs. Intervention to maintain the value of existing
property—*i.e.* to frustrate the effects of change in the
conditions of demand and supply—must cease. The
property owner must learn that only by continually
satisfying the demands of the consumer can he hope to
maintain intact its value. Only in such conditions can
we hope for the emergence of a structure of industry
which is stable in the sense that it can change without
recurrent catastrophe.

It is often said that this plea for the liberation of trade and investment to the domination of the market —that is, in the last resort, to the demand of the ultimate consumer—involves a denial of State functions, a demand for an anarchistic chaos. At the present day if it is desired to discredit any proposal, however modest, for the freeing of trade and industry, there is no more certain appeal to the gallery, no more certain title to the approval of the sciolist, than to say that it smacks of *laissez-faire*. If this essay should be reviewed by any of the more popular writers on these subjects, there is a 99 per cent probability that it will be said to be based upon a *laissez-faire* philosophy long since discredited among reasonable men, that it harks back to a system which is past, that it ignores the changed temper of the modern mind, and so on. What *laissez-faire* was; whether there ever was a *laissez-faire* philosophy in the sense usually implied; who discredited it—these are, of course, questions to which every intelligent man may be assumed to know the answer. They are questions therefore to which answers are never provided. Perhaps this is just as well. It is the emotional effect which is important.

In fact, of course, the propositions under discussion have no such implication. The plea that the market should be freed, and that private property should be left to assume the risks of investment and enterprise, in no way involves the denial of the economic functions of the State. Private property is itself a creation of the State. The delimitation of its scope and the maintenance of the appropriate mechanism of contract is a task of the utmost complexity, which can only be performed by the State. No one who has any idea of the nature of the problems relating, for instance, to the status of the so-called public utility undertakings under changing technical conditions can believe, for a moment, that in a world in which States abandoned all the specific measures of intervention which have here been the subject of discussion, their economic functions would cease to be of grave importance to the well-being of their citizens. In the context of this discussion the accusation of anarchism, of *laissez-faire*, of a denial of the economic functions of the State, is a pure red herring. All that is contended is that if the ends of stability and progress are deemed desirable, then States must abstain from certain forms of intervention which analysis most clearly shows to be definitely inimical to the achievement of these ends. To meet this indictment of a whole trend of policy with a smoke-screen of exceptional cases and metaphysical discussions of State functions is not argument: it is just obscurantism.

As a matter of fact, so far from such changes implying any abdication of the proper functions of the State, it is becoming increasingly clear that it is only in this way that their proper functions can be safeguarded. One of the most conspicuous and disquieting features of our time is the inefficiency of governmental institutions—not the inability of parliaments or dictatorships to "cure the depression"—they have already done so much curing as almost to kill the patient—but their inability to turn out laws which do not need to be revised within twelve months of their being placed on the statute book, their incapacity to pay sufficient attention to the great issues which States, and only States, can handle. The House of Commons, which, for good or for bad, is ultimately responsible for the government of India, can barely afford forty-eight hours in a normal year for the discussion of Indian business. The literature of political science abounds in discussions of this problem. The pundits are never tired of propounding new solutions in the shape of adjustments in the committee system, devolution on non-elected bodies, reform of local government, and so on. But it is essentially a problem which cannot be solved without a more radical limitation of State activity. The congestion of governmental business all over the world is due, in the last analysis, not to the trifling imperfections of this or that system or parliamentary procedure or to the absence of electric buttons for recording the votes of members, but to the fact that parliaments are assuming responsibility for more than they can properly supervise. The maxim "to govern well, govern little" is not to be interpreted in the sense that government is a necessary evil to be reduced to an absolute minimum, but in the sense that when governments bite off more than they can chew, they don't do their own business properly. The tendency to dictatorship in the modern world is an inevitable result of the fact that if democratic bodies attempt to go outside a certain sphere, either they do the business inefficiently or they abdicate their functions.

8. It has been the object of the last sections to show that if recovery is to be maintained and future progress assured, there must be a more or less complete reversal of contemporary tendencies of governmental regulation of enterprise. The aim of governmental policy in regard to industry must be to create a field in which the forces of enterprise and the disposal of resources are once more allowed to be governed by the market.

But what is this but the restoration of capitalism?

And is not the restoration of capitalism the restoration of the causes of depression?

If the analysis of this essay is correct, the answer is unequivocal. The conditions of recovery which have been stated do indeed involve the restoration of what has been called capitalism. But the slump was not due to these conditions. On the contrary, it was due to their negation. It was due to monetary mismanagement and State intervention operating in a *milieu* in which the essential strength of capitalism had already been sapped by war and by policy. Ever since the outbreak of war in 1914, the whole tendency of policy has been away from that system, which in spite of the persistence of feudal obstacles and the unprecedented multiplication of the people, produced that enormous increase of wealth per head which was characteristic of the period in which it was dominant. Whether that increase will be resumed, or whether, after perhaps some recovery, we shall be plunged anew into depression and the chaos of planning and restrictionism—that is the issue which depends on our willingness to reverse this tendency.

CHAPTER IX

1. WHAT, then, are the prospects of enduring recovery?

It is clear that they are not bright. It is quite probable, if there is no immediate outbreak of war on a large scale, that the next few months may see a substantial revival of business. If the exchanges are stabilised and the competition in depreciation ceases, there is a strong probability that the upward movement, which began in the summer of 1932, will continue. If the stabilisation were made permanent and some progress were made with the removal of the grosser obstacles to trade, it is not out of the question that a boom would develop. There are many things which might upset this development. The basis of recovery in the United States is gravely jeopardised by the policy of the Government. The conditions under which the dollar has been stabilised may lead to an inflation there, or most severe difficulties, financial and political, in continental Europe. There is the danger of war and civil disturbance.

These dangers may not mature. It may be that the next two or three years (or even longer) may be years of comparative revival. But it is impossible to feel any confidence in a continuance of stability. In the fifty years before the war, in England, a man planning his life on the threshold of his career might look forward to a time of reasonable peace and security, conditioned no doubt in part by the luck which governs so much even in the most settled society, but determined also by the vigour and the foresight with which he pursued his aims. To-day not even the most fortunate can have any such assurance. The probability of peace and progress in the next half-century is not very great. We may not feel this at every moment any more than we feel at every moment that we shall not live for ever. But the rational grounds for believing the contrary are not strong.

2. Why is this? There are two main reasons.

In the first place comes the danger of war. In the years immediately following the conclusion of the last war, the memory of what it meant and the relief at being delivered from its horrors, were so intense that most of us were loath to believe that such things could be allowed to occur again. There was never very much ground for this assurance, and recent events have made it clear that what ground there was has largely ceased to exist. So long as we could believe that the great body of people in civilised countries hated war and would be prepared to do anything to avoid it, it was possible to view the growing diplomatic tensions in Europe and elsewhere with the belief that these were minor difficulties which patience and goodwill could eliminate. The Nazi revolution has dispelled this illusion. We know now that, for a time at any rate, we have to live out our lives side by side with men whose conceptions of the true ends of life are fundamentally different from our own—men to whom the kindly virtues of peace are contemptible and for whom the destruction of life is a better thing than its preservation. We do damage to the prospects of peace if we fail to recognise this fact.

3. These paroxysms may pass. But the economic instability of the modern world does not seem likely to diminish. The tendencies making for instability, which we have examined in earlier chapters, have not been weakened during this depression. On the contrary, they have been strengthened. It is true that there are some signs of recognition of the mistakes which have been made in the sphere of monetary policy. But as yet there seems little will to repair them, still less to face the wider economic consequences which such repair would involve. For the rest, so far from there being any recognition of the instability and confusion which has been caused by the policy of interventionism, the majority of the leaders of public opinion seem to have drawn from the events of the last few years the conclusion that more intervention is necessary. All over the world, Governments to-day are actively engaged, on a scale unprecedented in history, in restricting trade and enterprise and undermining the basis of capitalism. Such a policy is not confined to the Socialists. Indeed the political power of the socialist parties in many parts of the world may be said to be waning. But their opponents, the dictators and the reactionaries, are inspired by the same ideas. It is a complete misapprehension to suppose that the victory of the Nazis and the Fascists is a defeat for the forces making for the destruction of capitalism. They have the same fanatical hatred of economic liberalism, the same hopes of a planned society. The differences are hierarchical. In Germany it is a crime deserving of torture or exile to be a Jew; in Russia to possess two cows. In our own more tranquil community the differences are equally non-economic. No doubt to their respective friends and colleagues it seems to make a world of difference

whether agriculture is planned by Major Elliot or Dr. Addison. From the economic point of view there is continuity of policy.

Such policies, as we have seen, have a cumulative tendency. They lead to an order of society which is likely to be less stable, less free, less productive, than our own. They lead, too, to an intensification of nationalism and to an enhancement of the causes which lead to civil strife. Men will not stand indefinitely a régime of catastrophic fluctuations. Neither will they acquiesce without blind protest in protracted impoverishment. We fail to realise the connection of things if we attribute the civil disorder and the nationalistic chaos of continental Europe entirely to the malevolence of violent men or the lack of foresight of the makers of treaties. The forces making for nationalism and domestic violence have no doubt been influenced by such factors. But they have been enormously strengthened by the results of economic policy. The unfortunate men who were shot down in the streets of Vienna the other day were the victims, not only of anti-democratic politics, they were the victims also of an economic policy which had eaten up the capital of industry, and by producing desperate impoverishment had provoked a violent reaction. It may be that in our more fortunate parts we have been given a period of respite. We have not yet travelled far down the Austrian road. But we deceive ourselves if we think we can stand indefinitely fluctuations of the present order of intensity.

4. It is often said that these developments are inevitable. The changes in policy which would be necessary to avert them are impossible, it is said, because men will not stand them. Whether we like it or not

the modern world is set upon the creation of the institutions and the habits which cause instability. Protest is unavailing. We can only go with the stream.

Such an attitude is surely unreasonable. If it can be shown, as has been argued in this essay, that the pursuance of these policies leads to instability and poverty, and if it can be shown too that these disasters are only to be avoided by the adoption of policies not favoured at the moment, then surely it is folly not to say so. It is not really to be believed that the majority of men in democratic communities are so in love with poverty and instability that if they were convinced that certain policies led in that direction they would continue to support them. On the contrary, it is clear that they at present support these policies because they believe —wrongly it has here been argued—that they lead to greater stability and progress. If they were convinced otherwise, can it be doubted that they would abandon them?

But can such things be in democratic communities? Can men be led by reason? Are not the majority of men so limited in outlook and so bound by prejudice that it is hopeless to endeavour to argue with them?

It is conceivable. But the history of the modern world does not bear out the contention. The policies which at present prevail have been adopted, not because they have been forced on politicians by the masses, but because the masses have been taught to believe them. The masses, as such, do not think for themselves; they think what they are taught to think by their leaders. And the ideas which, for good or for bad, have come to dominate policy are the ideas which have been put forward in the first instance by detached and isolated thinkers. If the direction of policy in

Great Britain, and the modern world generally, to-day
is overwhelmingly socialist, this is not because it is
dictated by the objective facts of the situation, or
because the masses with one accord have willed a
socialistic reorganisation of industry. It is because men
of intellect, with powers of reason and persuasion,
have conceived the socialistic idea and gradually persuaded their fellows. It is the same with monetary
policy. The measures of the last decade have been the
result, not of spontaneous pressure by the electorate,
but of the influence of a number of men whose names
could be counted on the fingers of two hands. We do
not appreciate fully the tragedy of this aspect of the
present situation unless we realise that it is essentially
the work of men of intellect and goodwill. In the short
run, it is true, ideas are unimportant and ineffective,
but in the long run they can rule the world.

There is, therefore, no reason to despair on the
ground that reason is necessarily powerless. It may
be that the forces, which have been released by the
ideas of forty years ago, have become so powerful—
so surcharged with mere mechanical impetus—that
it is now too late to arrest them. It would be unwise to
ignore the very strong probability that this is so. But
until the case, which experience and more recent
developments of knowledge have shown can be made
against them, has been argued with as much patience
and disinterested intelligence as went to the establishment of their ascendancy, we are not justified in concluding that reason and persuasion have reached the
limit of their effectiveness. At all events it is worth
trying.

STATISTICAL APPENDIX

TABLE I

UNITED KINGDOM

INDEX OF SECURITY PRICES

$(1926 = 100)$

Year and Month	Index	Year and Month	Index	Year and Month	Index
1925		**1928**		**1931**	
January .	96	January .	120	January .	84
February .	94	February .	119	February .	82
March	94	March	123	March	84
April .	94	April .	125	April .	82
May .	93	May .	129	May .	70
June .	93	June .	125	June .	72
July .	90	July .	121	July .	75
August	94	August	122	August	72
September .	95	September .	125	September .	68
October	98	October	128	October	76
November .	101	November .	125	November .	80
December .	99	December .	121	December .	71
1926		**1929**		**1932**	
January .	101	January .	130	January .	72
February .	100	February .	129	February .	70
March	99	March	125	March	75
April .	97	April .	125	April .	73
May .	99	May .	126	May .	67
June .	100	June .	123	June .	64
July .	99	July .	121	July .	73
August	100	August	124	August	75
September .	101	September .	126	September .	79
October	101	October	118	October	79
November .	102	November .	106	November .	80
December .	101	December .	106	December .	80
1927		**1930**		**1933**	
January .	105	January .	108	January .	83
February .	104	February .	104	February .	84
March	104	March	101	March	80
April .	104	April .	105	April .	81
May .	107	May .	104	May .	84
June .	107	June .	98	June .	88
July .	107	July .	98	July .	94
August	108	August	93	August	93
September .	110	September .	96	September .	96
October	114	October	90	October	100
November .	114	November .	92	November .	100
December .	114	December .	87	December .	99

The above index relates to the price of 92 ordinary industrial shares, the prices being taken on the 15th of each month. The index is based upon that of the *London and Cambridge Economic Service*, but the series has been recalculated from the original 1924 base for purposes of comparison with the American index.

TABLE 2

UNITED STATES

INDEX OF SECURITY PRICES

(1926 = 100)

Year and Month	Index	Year and Month	Index	Year and Month	Index
1925		**1928**		**1931**	
January .	83	January .	137	January .	103
February .	84	February .	135	February .	110
March	81	March	141	March .	112
April . .	80	April . .	150	April . .	100
May . .	83	May . .	155	May . .	89
June . .	85	June . .	148	June . .	87
July . .	88	July . .	148	July . .	90
August .	89	August .	153	August .	89
September .	92	September .	162	September .	76
October .	96	October .	166	October .	65
November .	100	November .	179	November .	68
December .	100	December .	178	December .	54
1926		**1929**		**1932**	
January .	102	January .	193	January .	54
February .	102	February .	192	February .	53
March .	96	March .	196	March .	54
April . .	93	April . .	193	April . .	42
May . .	93	May . .	193	May . .	38
June . .	97	June . .	191	June . .	34
July . .	100	July . .	203	July . .	36
August .	103	August .	210	August .	52
September .	104	September .	216	September .	56
October .	102	October .	194	October .	48
November .	103	November .	145	November .	45
December .	105	December .	147	December .	45
1927		**1930**		**1933**	
January .	106	January .	149	January .	46
February .	108	February .	156	February .	43
March .	109	March .	163	March .	42
April . .	110	April . .	171	April . .	49
May . .	113	May . .	160	May . .	65
June . .	114	June . .	143	June . .	77
July . .	117	July . .	140	July . .	84
August .	122	August .	139	August .	79
September .	129	September .	139	September .	81
October .	128	October .	118	October .	76
November .	131	November .	109	November .	77
December .	136	December .	102	December .	79

This index, compiled by the *Standard Statistics Company*, is based on 335-351 ordinary industrial shares, the average of the closing prices on each Thursday of the month being used.

TABLE 3

TOTAL CAPITAL ISSUES

Year and Month	United Kingdom		United States		Year and Month	United Kingdom		United States	
	Amount	*Index*	Amount	*Index*		Amount	*Index*	Amount	*Index*
	£ millions	*1929 =100*	$ millions	*1929 =100*		£ millions	*1929 =100*	$ millions	*1929 =100*
1929					1932				
Jan.	47·4	*225*	915	*121*	Jan.	2·9	*14*	180	*24*
Feb.	33·0	*156*	894	*118*	Feb.	12·0	*57*	74	*10*
Mar.	33·8	*160*	984	*130*	Mar.	12·1	*57*	162	*21*
April	34·8	*165*	677	*89*	April	18·0	*85*	71	*9*
May	21·1	*100*	1127	*149*	May	12·3	*58*	91	*12*
June	25·4	*120*	773	*102*	June	17·5	*83*	84	*11*
July	22·2	*105*	880	*116*	July	3·3	*16*	105	*14*
Aug.	3·6	*17*	843	*111*	Aug.	0·1	··	62	*8*
Sept.	2·7	*13*	307	*40*	Sept.	··	··	93	*12*
Oct.	11·5	*54*	843	*111*	Oct.	19·7	*93*	98	*13*
Nov.	12·9	*61*	281	*37*	Nov.	10·8	*51*	44	*6*
Dec.	5·3	*25*	574	*76*	Dec.	4·3	*20*	123	*16*
1930					1933				
Jan.	16·9	*80*	747	*99*	Jan.	8·3	*39*	65	*9*
Feb.	26·2	*124*	598	*79*	Feb.	7·2	*34*	20	*3*
Mar.	26·4	*125*	799	*105*	Mar.	13·4	*63*	16	*2*
April	21·3	*101*	903	*119*	April	8·2	*39*	25	*3*
May	37·9	*179*	1109	*146*	May	14·6	*69*	44	*6*
June	13·2	*62*	704	*93*	June	17·5	*83*	110	*15*
July	16·4	*78*	553	*73*	July	6·0	*28*	117	*15*
Aug.	6·6	*31*	204	*27*	Aug.	21·2	*100*	46	*6*
Sept.	5·0	*24*	379	*50*	Sept.	7·2	*34*	64	*8*
Oct.	30·5	*144*	394	*52*	Oct.	10·0	*47*	59	*8*
Nov.	19·9	*94*	258	*34*	Nov.	12·8	*61*	88	*12*
Dec.	15·9	*75*	385	*51*	Dec.	6·4	*30*	57	*8*
1931									
Jan.	12·3	*58*	466	*61*					
Feb.	19·6	*93*	206	*27*					
Mar.	13·4	*63*	560	*74*					
April	1·7	*8*	368	*49*					
May	11·0	*52*	341	*45*					
June	12·8	*61*	250	*33*					
July	5·2	*25*	226	*30*					
Aug.	1·7	*8*	120	*16*					
Sept.	1·3	*6*	268	*35*					
Oct.	2·5	*12*	44	*6*					
Nov.	4·4	*21*	109	*14*					
Dec.	2·7	*13*	119	*16*					

The series for the United States is published by the *Commercial and Financial Chronicle*. The monthly average for 1929, upon which the index is based, is $758 millions.

The United Kingdom series was compiled by the *Midland Bank*, and the figures are for "subscriptions invited on the home market, excluding Government loans for national purposes, local government loans with no specific limit to total subscriptions and bonds of less than 12 months currency". The monthly average for 1929 is £21·1 millions.

TABLE 4

Capital Issues on Foreign Account

Year and Month	United Kingdom		United States		Year and Month	United Kingdom		United States	
	Amount	Index	Amount	Index		Amount	Index	Amount	Index
1929	£ millions	1929 =100	$ millions	1929 =100	1932	£ millions	1929 =100	$ millions	1929 =100
Jan.	29·4	374	40	63	Jan.	2·6	33	..	..
Feb.	6·9	88	66	104	Feb.	2·9	37	..	..
Mar.	9·0	114	225	354	Mar.	1·0	13	..	..
April	6·0	76	16	25	April	8·4	107	..	..
May	8·8	112	47	74	May	3·4	43	..	..
June	11·4	145	172	270	June	2·1	27	..	..
July	8·3	105	35	55	July	0·1	1	..	..
Aug.	1·4	18	21	33	Aug.	..	..	2	3
Sept.	1·2	15	8	13	Sept.	..	..	20	31
Oct.	4·1	52	53	83	Oct.	7·9	100	4	6
Nov.	6·7	85	35	55	Nov.	0·5	6	1	2
Dec.	1·2	15	45	71	Dec.	0·3	4	..	..
1930					1933				
Jan.	5·6	71	31	49	Jan.	0·4	5	..	..
Feb.	18·2	231	126	198	Feb.	2·3	29	..	..
Mar.	9·4	119	141	222	Mar.	1·2	15	..	..
April	9·4	119	175	275	April	1·0	13	..	..
May	20·1	255	120	189	May	5·3	67	..	..
June	5·5	70	176	277	June	1·5	19	..	..
July	3·3	42	80	126	July	0·8	10	1	2
Aug.	3·1	39	39	61	Aug.	19·9	253	..	..
Sept.	2·6	33	3	5	Sept.	0·4	5	..	..
Oct.	17·7	225	100	157	Oct.	3·2	41	..	..
Nov.	8·4	107	10	16	Nov.	0·6	7	..	..
Dec.	5·4	69	21	33	Dec.	1·3	17	..	..
1931									
Jan.	4·5	57	132	208					
Feb.	13·7	174	4	6					
Mar.	6·0	76	10	16					
April	0·3	4	..	..					
May	10·1	128	8	13					
June	8·5	108	26	41					
July	2·9	37	..	..					
Aug.	..	..	..	..					
Sept.	..	..	51	80					
Oct.	..	..	..	..					
Nov.	..	..	..	..					
Dec.	..	..	..	..					

The data for the United States are published by the *Commercial and Financial Chronicle*, and the monthly average for 1929 upon which the index is based is $63·6 millions.

The United Kingdom series was compiled by the *Midland Bank*, and the monthly average for 1929 is £7·87 millions.

TABLE 5

UNITED KINGDOM—INDEX OF WHOLESALE PRICES

(1913 = 100)

Month	1921	1922	1923	1924	1925	1926	1927	1928	1929	1930	1931	1932	1933
January	251·0	164·0	157·1	165·4	171·1	150·1	143·6	141·1	138·4	131·0	106·9	106·0	100·3
February	229·9	161·8	157·6	167·0	168·9	147·6	142·6	140·3	138·4	127·8	106·2	105·4	98·9
March	215·1	159·9	160·3	165·4	166·3	144·3	140·6	140·8	140·1	124·5	105·9	104·7	97·6
April	208·7	159·8	162·0	164·7	162·5	143·6	139·8	142·9	138·8	123·7	105·7	102·4	97·2
May	205·0	160·4	159·9	163·7	159·0	144·9	141·1	143·6	135·8	122·0	104·4	100·7	99·2
June	201·6	159·7	159·5	162·6	157·6	146·4	141·8	142·6	135·6	120·7	103·2	98·0	101·7
July	198·2	159·9	156·7	162·6	157·5	148·7	141·1	141·1	137·4	119·2	102·2	97·7	102·3
August	193·9	155·8	154·7	165·2	157·0	149·1	140·9	139·3	135·8	117·8	99·5	99·6	102·5
September	191·0	153·9	158·0	166·9	156·0	150·9	142·1	137·6	135·8	115·5	99·2	102·1	103·0
October	184·4	154·8	158·3	170·0	154·8	152·1	141·4	137·9	136·1	113·0	104·4	101·1	102·6
November	176·4	157·1	161·1	169·8	153·7	152·4	141·1	137·9	134·0	112·0	106·4	101·1	102·8
December	167·9	155·8	163·4	170·1	152·1	146·1	140·4	138·2	132·5	108·9	105·8	101·0	102·8

The above indices are monthly averages, the source being the Board of Trade.

TABLE 6

UNITED STATES—INDEX OF WHOLESALE PRICES

(1926 = 100)

Month	1921	1922	1923	1924	1925	1926	1927	1928	1929	1930	1931	1932	1933
January	114	91	102	100	103	103	97	96	96	93	78	67	61
February	105	93	103	100	104	102	96	96	95	91	77	66	60
March	102	93	104	99	104	101	95	96	96	90	76	66	60
April	99	93	104	97	102	100	94	97	96	90	75	66	60
May	96	96	102	96	102	101	94	98	95	89	73	64	63
June	93	96	100	95	103	100	94	97	95	87	72	64	65
July	93	99	98	96	104	100	94	97	97	84	72	65	69
August	94	99	98	97	104	99	95	98	96	84	72	65	70
September	93	99	100	97	103	100	96	99	96	84	71	65	71
October	94	100	99	98	104	99	97	97	95	83·	70	64	71
November	94	101	98	99	105	98	96	96	94	81	70	64	71
December	93	101	98	102	103	98	96	96	93	80	69	63	71

The above indices are monthly averages, the series having been compiled by the *Bureau of Labour Statistics* from 784 separate series of wholesale prices.

TABLE 7

INDICES OF THE COST OF LIVING

(July 1914 = 100)

Year and Month	United Kingdom	United States	Year and Month	United Kingdom	United States
1929			**1932**		
January .	165	161	January .	147	130
February .	166	161	February .	146	128
March. .	162	160	March .	144	127
April . .	161	159	April . .	143	126
May . .	160	159	May . .	142	124
June . .	161	160	June . .	143	123
July . .	163	162	July . .	141	123
August .	164	163	August .	141	123
September .	165	163	September .	143	122
October .	167	163	October .	143	121
November .	167	163	November .	143	121
December .	166	162	December .	142	120
1930			**1933**		
January .	164	160	January .	141	118
February .	161	159	February .	139	115
March. .	157	157	March .	137	115
April . .	155	158	April . .	136	114
May . .	154	156	May . .	136	116
June . .	155	155	June . .	138	116
July . .	157	152	July . .	139	120
August .	157	152	August .	141	123
September .	156	153	September .	141	124
October .	157	152	October .	143	125
November .	155	150	November .	143	124
December .	153	148 —[1]	December .	142	123
1931					
January .	152	145			
February .	150	143			
March. .	147	142			
April . .	147	141			
May . .	145	139			
June . .	147	137			
July . .	145	137			
August .	145	137			
September .	145	137			
October .	146	135			
November :	148	134			
December .	147	133			

The figures for the United States are for the middle of the month; for the United Kingdom, end of the month. In both cases, the base is July 1914.

[1] After this point the figures given are those of the *National Industrial Conference Board* converted from the 1923 base. Strict comparability is not possible between the two sections of the series and there is reason to suppose that they would diverge appreciably.

TABLE 8

INDICES OF INDUSTRIAL PRODUCTION

(1928 = 100)

Year and Month	Germany	U.K.	U.S.A.	Year and Month	Germany	U.K.	U.S.A.
1929				**1932**			
January .	95	..	105	January .	62	..	65
February .	91	106	105	February .	63	89	62
March .	99	..	106	March .	61	..	60
April .	108	..	110	April .	61	..	57
May .	109	108	111	May .	62	81	54
June .	110	..	114	June .	61	..	53
July .	105	..	112	July .	60	..	52
August .	104	106	111	August .	59	76	54
September	102	..	110	September	60	..	60
October .	101	..	105	October .	61	..	60
November	101	112	96	November.	62	85	59
December	96	..	89	December .	62	..	60
1930				**1933**			
January .	95	..	94	January .	63	..	59
February .	93	107	97	February .	65	86	57
March .	93	..	94	March .	65	..	54
April .	95	..	96	April .	66	..	60
May .	90	98	94	May .	68	87	70
June .	84	..	90	June .	70	..	83
July .	81	..	85	July .	71	..	90
August .	80	89	83	August .	71	86	82
September	78	..	82	September	71	..	76
October .	77	..	79	October .	72	..	69
November	76	90	76	November.	73	95	65
December	72	..	74	December .	75	..	68
1931							
January .	68	..	74				
February .	69	83	78				
March .	74	..	78				
April .	76	..	80				
May .	74	79	80				
June .	74	..	76				
July .	72	..	75				
August .	68	79	71				
September	67	..	69				
October .	64	..	66				
November	64	88	65				
December	60	..	67				

The above statistics have been compiled from the bulletins of the German *Institut für Konjunkturforschung*.
The original sources are:
GERMANY—Institut für Konjunkturforschung.
U.K.—London and Cambridge Economic Service (original base, 1924).
U.S.A.—Federal Reserve Board (original base, 1923–1925).

TABLE 9

INDICES OF PRODUCTION OF PRODUCERS' AND
CONSUMERS' GOODS

(1925–1929 = 100)

Year or Quarter	PRODUCERS' GOODS			CONSUMERS' GOODS		
	Germany	U.K.	U.S.A.	Germany	U.K.	U.S.A.
1925	88	..	93	87	..	97
1926	85	..	99	89	..	97
1927	108	102	92	111	101	102
1928	107	100	104	109	100	100
1929	112	107	113	104	100	104
1930	95	96	83	101	90	88
1931	70	78	54	94	88	89
1932	54	75	29	85	90	82
1930: (1)	108	108	97	103	95	95
(2)	98	102	92	103	90	88
(3)	90	93	78	99	87	85
(4)	85	84	63	99	90	87
1931: (1)	77	83	66	92	85	88
(2)	76	80	60	98	87	91
(3)	71	73	47	94	89	92
(4)	58	77	42	91	96	87
1932: (1)	54	78	36	86	92	84
(2)	55	77	27	84	93	70
(3)	52	72	24	83	85	84
(4)	54	75	28	86	90	87
1933: (1)	58	77	25	85	89	82

Compiled from the League of Nations' *World Production and Prices, 1925–32*, Table V. p. 56.

GERMANY—*Producers'* industries include: iron and steel, non-ferrous ores and metals, building, machinery, motor vehicles, shipbuilding, coal, petroleum, gas, electricity, paper, hemp, yarn and potash. *Consumers'* industries include: textiles, footwear, glassware, porcelain, musical instruments, meat, dairy produce, sugar, tobacco products, beer, brandy, sea fishes.

UNITED STATES.—*Investment* industries represented by iron and steel, tin and cement. *Consumers'* industries represented by textiles, leather and food industries.

UNITED KINGDOM.—*Investment* industries represented by iron and steel, non-ferrous metals, chemicals, engineering and shipbuilding. *Consumers'* industries as in the case of U.S.A.

TABLE 10

TOTAL VALUE OF WORLD TRADE

(1929–1932)

Millions of Dollars

Year	Imports	Exports	Total
1929	35,606	33,035	68,641
1930	29,083	26,492	55,575
1931	20,847	18,922	39,769
1932	13,885	12,726	26,611

From the League of Nations' *World Economic Survey, 1932–33*, p. 211.

TABLE 11

NATIONAL UNEMPLOYMENT STATISTICS

END OF MARCH [1]

(In thousands)

Country	1929	1930	1931	1932	1933
Australia.	39	63	114	120	109
Austria	225	239	304	417	456
Belgium [2]	28	42	207	350	383
Canada	12	23	32	77	80
Czechoslovakia	50	88	340	634	878
Danzig	18	20	27	36	38
Denmark	66	49	70	145	166
Esthonia	4	4	3	8	15
Finland	3	10	11	18	19
France	9	14	72	347	356
Germany.	2.484	3,041	4,744	6,034	5,599
Hungary	14	43	55	71	69
Irish Free State [4]	19	23	25	31	83
Italy [2]	309	413	735	1,085	1,111
Japan	..	352	397	474	..
Latvia	9	6	9	23	13
Netherlands	..	..	..	253	342
New Zealand	3	3	38	45	51
Norway	24	23	29	38	42
Poland	177	289	373	360	280
Roumania	10	13	48	55	..
Saar	9	9	18	45	42
Sweden	44	42	73	99	121
Switzerland [2]	9	21	61	103	113
United Kingdom [2]	1,204	1,694	2,666	2,660	2,821
United States [3]	..	2,964	6,403	10,477	13,359
Yugoslavia	12	10	12	23	23

Reproduced from the League of Nations' *World Economic Survey 1932–33*, p. 109.

[1] Original Source—League of Nations' *Monthly Bulletin of Statistics.*

[2] Partial and intermittent unemployment included.

[3] Figures for United States, 1930–1932 ; American Federation of Labour, see *Weltwirtschaftliches Archiv*, April 1933.

[4] New Series from June 1932.

THE GREAT DEPRESSION

TABLE 12

UNITED STATES

INDEX OF INDUSTRIAL PRODUCTION

(1923–1925 = 100)

Year and Month	Index	Year and Month	Index	Year and Month	Index
1925		**1928**		**1931**	
January .	105	January .	105	January .	82
February .	107	February .	111	February .	87
March .	107	March .	112	March .	89
April . .	104	April . .	110	April . .	90
May . .	103	May . .	110	May . .	89
June . .	100	June . .	108	June . .	83
July . .	99	July . .	105	July . .	80
August .	101	August .	110	August .	78
September .	102	September .	116	September .	77
October .	107	October .	118	October .	75
November .	108	November .	115	November .	73
December .	103	December .	109	December .	68
1926		**1929**		**1932**	
January .	105	January .	117	January .	71
February .	108	February .	121	February .	71
March .	110	March .	124	March .	68
April . .	108	April . .	124	April . .	64
May . .	107	May . .	126	May . .	61
June . .	106	June . .	125	June . .	59
July . .	103	July . .	120	July . .	56
August .	109	August .	122	August .	59
September .	113	September .	123	September .	67
October .	114	October .	121	October .	68
November .	110	November .	108	November .	65
December .	101	December .	96	December .	60
1927		**1930**		**1933**	
January .	106	January .	103	January .	64
February .	111	February .	109	February .	64
March .	113	March .	106	March .	60
April . .	110	April . .	107	April : .	67
May . .	112	May . .	105	May . .	79
June . .	107	June . .	99	June . .	91
July . .	102	July . .	91	July . .	96
August .	105	August .	90	August .	90
September .	106	September .	92	September .	85
October .	105	October .	90	October .	78
November .	101	November .	84	November .	72
December .	96	December .	77	December .	69

The above index has been compiled by the *Federal Reserve Board, Division of Research and Statistics,* from 57 individual series of data representing the production of about 34 industries and estimated to represent directly, or indirectly, about 80 per cent of total industrial production in the United States. The base is the monthly average for the years 1923 to 1925.

TABLE 13

UNITED STATES

ACCEPTANCES AND SECURITIES OF FEDERAL RESERVE

BANKS

Millions of Dollars

Year and Month	Accept- ances and Securities	Year and Month	Accept- ances and Securities	Year and Month	Accept- ances and Securities
1929		**1931**		**1933**	
January .	702	January .	853	January .	1838
February.	569	February.	705	February.	1906
March .	462	March .	727	March .	2254
April .	321	April .	773	April .	2067
May .	298	May .	743	May .	1932
June .	278	June .	731	June .	1945
July .	222	July .	753	July .	2032
August .	279	August .	847	August .	2072
September	394	September	995	September	2209
October .	491	October .	1425	October .	2362
November	611	November	1287	November	2452
December	766	December	1117	December	2533
1930		**1932**			
January .	799	January .	980		
February.	765	February.	894		
March .	786	March .	914		
April .	796	April .	1066		
May .	711	May .	1454		
June .	712	June .	1747		
July .	737	July .	1878		
August .	752	August .	1887		
September	794	September	1882		
October .	787	October .	1885		
November	783	November	1885		
December	901	December	1888		

These are monthly averages of daily figures, and represent the total acceptances and securities of the Federal Reserve Banks. The series has been compiled from the *Federal Reserve Bulletin*.

TABLE 14

BANK OF ENGLAND

TOTAL DEPOSITS

Millions Sterling

Year and Month	Deposits	Year and Month	Deposits	Year and Month	Deposits
1925		**1928**		**1931**	
January .	129·8	January .	115·2	January .	107·9
February .	121·7	February .	108·6	February .	108·6
March .	121·4	March .	111·9	March .	100·9
April .	122·5	April .	112·8	April .	103·7
May .	122·5	May .	111·8	May .	106·0
June .	131·8	June .	129·5	June .	120·4
July .	124·0	July .	118·4	July .	104·7
August .	126·0	August .	114·5	August .	128·6
September	129·5	September	113·4	September	145·3
October .	113·7	October .	117·7	October .	133·4
November	125·7	November .	121·0	November .	125·0
December .	169·0	December .	120·0	December .	174·4
1926		**1929**		**1932**	
January .	123·9	January .	115·3	January .	127·8
February .	122·2	February .	107·7	February .	114·2
March .	129·0	March .	114·3	March .	116·1
April .	114·6	April .	112·4	April .	117·0
May .	123·3	May .	115·6	May .	134·1
June .	165·1	June .	128·3	June .	139·3
July .	115·2	July .	109·1	July .	133·9
August .	128·2	August .	114·6	August .	135·7
September	122·4	September	108·1	September	137·4
October .	122·6	October .	110·6	October .	136·3
November	124·6	November .	113·8	November .	137·7
December .	143·0	December .	115·6	December .	145·1
1927		**1930**		**1933**	
January .	116·5	January .	118·1	January .	147·5
February .	116·3	February .	98·9	February .	159·5
March .	130·4	March .	109·6	March .	148·9
April .	108·8	April .	123·7	April .	148·8
May .	118·1	May .	108·1	May .	150·2
June .	126·9	June .	121·4	June .	161·4
July .	113·4	July .	107·5	July .	170·3
August .	115·3	August .	114·6	August .	164·4
September	123·2	September	111·6	September	157·8
October .	111·8	October .	111·7	October .	165·8
November	113·6	November .	111·6	November .	157·0
December .	138·5	December .	175·2	December .	159·9

The above figures relate to the end of the month and comprise:
  (a) "Public Deposits" (including Exchequer, Savings Banks, Commissioners of National Debt, and Dividend Accounts).
  (b) "Private Deposits" ("Bankers' Deposits" and "Other Accounts").

TABLE 15

UNITED STATES

VELOCITY OF CIRCULATION OF BANK DEPOSITS [1]

Year and Month	Deposits [2] $ millions	Debits [3] $ millions	Ratio	Year and Month	Deposits [2] $ millions	Debits [3] $ millions	Ratio
1926				**1930**			
January .	29,169	54,145	1·86	January .	31,982	60,423	1·89
February	29,149	44,915	1·54	February	31,531	52,625	1·67
March .	28,984	56,464	1·95	March .	31,791	65,723	2·07
April .	29,112	51,837	1·78	April .	32,159	62,946	1·96
May .	29,240	48,020	1·64	May .	32,229	61,811	1·92
June .	29,287	50,662	1·73	June .	32,504	62,312	1·92
July .	29,393	50,959	1·73	July .	32,663	52,744	1·61
August .	29,385	47,011	1·60	August .	32,581	45,993	1·41
September	29,586	46,954	1·59	September	32,643	48,636	1·49
October .	29,682	52,535	1·77	October .	32,726	54,460	1·66
November	29,654	47,384	1·60	November	33,014	42,176	1·28
December	29,825	57,070	1·91	December	32,314	52,107	1·61
1927				**1931**			
January .	29,729	54,714	1·84	January .	32,048	46,253	1·44
February	29,900	48,220	1·61	February	31,968	38,031	1·19
March .	30,257	58,518	1·93	March .	32,069	47,011	1·47
April .	30,348	55,583	1·83	April .	32,179	46,440	1·44
May .	30,595	54,143	1·77	May .	32,168	43,930	1·37
June .	30,693	56,820	1·85	June .	31,602	45,299	1·43
July .	30,816	53,682	1·74	July .	31,526	39,451	1·25
August .	30,827	53,702	1·74	August .	31,041	34,027	1·10
September	31,119	56,750	1·82	September	30,500	36,700	1·20
October .	31,487	59,201	1·88	October .	29,138	38,802	1·33
November	31,759	57,085	1·80	November	28,218	29,069	1·03
December	32,263	65,441	2·03	December	27,438	36,345	1·32
1928				**1932**			
January .	32,263	62,885	1·95	January .	26,592	33,569	1·26
February	32,647	54,493	1·67	February	25,715	27,251	1·06
March .	32,153	70,633	2·20	March .	25,431	29,889	1·18
April .	32,165	67,003	2·08	April .	25,386	29,923	1·18
May .	32,650	71,616	2·19	May .	25,466	25,411	1·00
June .	32,735	72,485	2·21	June .	25,075	27,103	1·08
July .	32,613	58,981	1·81	July .	24,712	25,239	1·02
August .	32,211	58,504	1·82	August .	24,744	25,215	1·02
September	31,651	63,176	2·00	September	24,973	25,931	1·04
October .	32,059	72,894	2·27	October .	25,292	25,298	1·00
November	32,241	71,349	2·21	November	25,476	20,750	0·81
December	32,578	82,386	2·53	December	25,492	26,787	1·05
1929				**1933**			
January .	32,566	82,814	2·54	January .	25,641	24,466	0·95
February	32,298	70,777	2·19	February	24,978	22,437	0·90
March .	32,068	83,524	2·60	March .	. . [4]	. . [4]	
April .	31,794	74,750	2·35	April .	21,710	22,628	1·04
May .	31,733	76,535	2·41	May .	22,509	25,486	1·13
June .	31,761	69,666	2·19	June .	22,974	29,711	1·29
July .	31,921	77,631	2·43	July .	23,160	31,232	1·35
August .	31,896	77,344	2·42	August .	23,039	25,451	1·10
September	32,090	77,617	2·42	September	23,140	24,555	1·06
October .	32,441	95,572	2·95	October	23,369	26,307	1·13
November	33,173	82,090	2·47	November	23,486	24,131	1·03
December	32,182	66,752	2·07	December	23,646	26,301	1·11

[1] Ratio of Bank Debits each month to the average of Bank Deposits for the same month. What is significant is not the absolute magnitude of this figure but its fluctuations through time.

[2] Net Demand Deposits plus Time Deposits of all member banks: Monthly averages.

[3] Debits in 141 Federal Reserve Cities: Monthly totals.

[4] Licensed Banks only, after this date. The data relating to Deposits and Debits has been compiled from the *Federal Reserve Bulletin*.

THE GREAT DEPRESSION

TABLE 16

UNITED STATES

TOTAL GOLD RESERVES OF THE FEDERAL RESERVE BANKS

Millions of Dollars

Year and Month	Gold Reserves	Year and Month	Gold Reserves	Year and Month	Gold Reserves
1926		**1929**		**1932**	
January	2801	January	2657	January	2976
February	2767	February	2677	February	2938
March	2767	March	2701	March	3020
April	2797	April	2791	April	3004
May	2816	May	2813	May	2790
June	2835	June	2858	June	2578
July	2851	July	2924	July	2635
August	2841	August	2945	August	2773
September	2807	September	2971	September	2893
October	2823	October	3004	October	3003
November	2830	November	2948	November	3049
December	2815	December	2857	December	3151
1927		**1930**		**1933**	
January	2967	January	2960	January	3256
February	2983	February	2965	February	2952
March	3022	March	3015	March	3250
April	3041	April	3073	April	3416
May	3002	May	3038	May	3520
June	3021	June	3012	June	3543
July	3023	July	2990	July	3548
August	2998	August	2927	August	3588
September	2989	September	2967	September	3591
October	2957	October	3004	October	3591
November	2805	November	2981	November	3573
December	2739	December	2941	December	3569
1928		**1931**			
January	2819	January	3062		
February	2808	February	3070		
March	2760	March	3115		
April	2723	April	3161		
May	2607	May	3250		
June	2583	June	3409		
July	2604	July	3431		
August	2619	August	3456		
September	2633	September	3138		
October	2641	October	2746		
November	2600	November	2918		
December	2584	December	2989		

These figures, which do not include gold earmarked for foreign account, have been compiled from the *Federal Reserve Bulletin* and relate to the last Wednesday of each month. It would appear that strictly comparable data will not be available in future.

TABLE 17

UNITED STATES

TOTAL LOANS, DISCOUNTS AND INVESTMENTS OF WEEKLY REPORTING MEMBER BANKS

Millions of Dollars

Year and Month	Loans, Discounts and Investments	Year and Month	Loans, Discounts and Investments	Year and Month	Loans, Discounts and Investments
1926		**1929**		**1932**	
January .	19,426	Januar .	22,320	January .	20,178
February .	19,422	Februai y .	22,263	February .	19,775
March .	19,546	March .	22,472	March .	19,434
April .	19,525	April .	22,388	April .	19,096
May .	19,579	May .	22,114	May .	19,112
June .	19,816	June .	22,231	June .	18,877
July .	19,627	July .	22,479	July .	18,419
August .	19,684	August .	22,465	August .	18,587
September	20,029	September	22,646	September	18,739
October .	19,892	October .	23,124	October .	19,026
November	19,849	November.	23,663	November.	18,987
December .	20,110	December .	23,012	December .	18,840
1927		**1930**		**1933**	
January .	19,686	January .	22,368	January .	18,665
February .	19,558	February .	22,083	February .	18,532
March .	19,989	March .	22,352		
April .	20,068	April .	22,657		
May .	20,273	May .	22,662		
June .	20,506	June .	23,024		
July .	20,404	July .	23,101		
August .	20,357	August .	23,128		
September	20,653	September	23,220		
October .	20,918	October .	23,409		
November	21,112	November.	23,455		
December .	21,328	December .	23,117		
1928		**1931**			
January .	21,493	January .	22,660		
February .	21,315	February .	22,659		
March .	21,502	March .	22,839		
April .	21,944	April .	22,942		
May .	22,148	May .	22,713		
June .	22,063	June .	22,439		
July .	22,006	July .	22,393		
August .	21,809	August .	22,093		
September	21,871	September	22,078		
October .	21,938	October .	21,425		
November	21,983	November.	21,023		
December .	22,189	December.	20,749		

The above figures are monthly averages, except for the year 1926, when they related to the last return of the month. Strictly comparable figures are not available after February 1933. The series has been compiled from the *Federal Reserve Bulletin.*

TABLE 18

BANK OF FRANCE

GOLD RESERVES AND NOTES IN CIRCULATION

Millions of Francs

Year and Month	Gold Reserves plus Foreign Assets	Notes in Circulation	Year and Month	Gold Reserves plus Foreign Assets	Notes in Circulation
1928			October .	65,954	68,246
June .	56,235	60,628	November	66,633	68,159
July .	59,353	60,434	December .	67,439	67,149
August .	62,301	62,184			
September	61,765	62,654	**1930**		
October .	63,263	61,327	January .	68,611	70,339
November	62,275	62,660	February .	68,525	71,116
December	64,618	63,916	March .	68,192	70,826
			April .	67,946	72,373
1929			May .	69,336	73,079
January .	64,451	62,153	June .	69,654	72,594
February	63,860	62,506	July .	72,046	74,008
March .	63,078	64,575	August .	72,818	73,677
April .	62,813	62,848	September	74,001	73,053
May .	62,788	64,316	October .	76,399	74,787
June .	62,357	64,921	November	77,834	75,951
July .	63,103	64,135	December .	79,725	76,436
August .	64,732	66,467			
September	65,225	66,639			

The above figures, compiled from the *Annuaire Statistique de la France*, relate to the end of each month. Comparable statistics are not available before June 1928, the gold reserves of the Bank of France having been revalued at that date.

TABLE 19

BANK OF ENGLAND

GOLD RESERVES

Millions Sterling

Year and Month	Gold Reserves	Year and Month	Gold Reserves	Year and Month	Gold Reserves
1925		**1928**		**1931**	
January .	155·6	January .	155·9	January .	140·1
February .	155·6	February .	157·3	February .	141·6
March .	155·7	March .	158·1	March .	144·5
April .	155·7	April .	160·7	April .	147·2
May .	156·5	May .	162·9	May .	152·1
June .	157·6	June .	172·3	June .	164·0
July .	164·3	July .	173·7	July .	133·3
August .	162·5	August .	175·9	August .	134·6
September	160·5	September	173·2	September	136·1
October .	150·3	October .	164·9	October .	136·9
November	145·7	November	159·8	November	121·7
December .	144·6	December .	153·3	December .	121·3
1926.		**1929**		**1932**	
January .	144·5	January .	153·0	January .	121·4
February .	144·6	February .	151·3	February .	121·3
March .	146·8	March .	153·7	March .	121·4
April .	146·4	April .	158·8	April .	121·5
May .	148·8	May .	163·3	May .	125·8
June .	150·3	June .	155·7	June .	137·0
July .	152·1	July .	142·6	July .	138·6
August .	155·5	August .	137·6	August .	139·8
September	155·8	September	130·3	September	140·4
October .	152·8	October .	132·1	October .	140·4
November	152·9	November	135·4	November	140·4
December .	151·1	December .	146·1	December .	120·6
1927		**1930**		**1933**	
January .	151·0	January .	150·4	January .	124·4
February .	150·1	February .	152·0	February .	143·0
March .	150·5	March .	157·1	March .	172·7
April .	154·2	April .	164·3	April .	186·9
May .	152·6	May .	158·1	May .	187·4
June .	152·1	June .	157·2	June .	190·6
July .	151·8	July .	153·3	July .	191·4
August .	151·2	August .	155·9	August .	191·7
September	151·1	September	156·8	September	191·8
October .	151·3	October .	160·7	October .	191·8
November	149·9	November	155·6	November	191·8
December .	152·4	December .	148·3	December .	191·7

The above figures relate to the end of the month and, for the year 1925, include gold in the Treasury. Since September 1931 an additional quantity of gold (of unknown amount) has been held by the Exchange Equalisation Account.

TABLE 20

LONDON CLEARING BANKS

TOTAL DEPOSITS

Millions Sterling

Year and Month	Deposits	Year and Month	Deposits	Year and Month	Deposits
1925		**1928**		**1931**	
January .	1653	January .	1747	January .	1836
February .	1643	February .	1698	February .	1782
March .	1605	March .	1672	March .	1726
April .	1606	April .	1690	April .	1698
May .	1598	May .	1688	May .	1700
June .	1624	June .	1731	June .	1744
July .	1633	July .	1749	July .	1750
August .	1611	August .	1732	August .	1708
September	1613	September	1732	September	1675
October .	1627	October .	1753	October .	1688
November	1619	November.	1752	November.	1670
December .	1647	December .	1806	December .	1700
1926		**1929**		**1932**	
January .	1637	January .	1809	January .	1677
February .	1606	February .	1777	February .	1621
March .	1588	March .	1739	March .	1639
April .	1590	April .	1743	April .	1643
May .	1590	May .	1732	May .	1661
June .	1630	June .	1770	June .	1727
July .	1646	July .	1778	July .	1765
August .	1634	August .	1759	August .	1813
September	1623	September	1754	September	1826
October .	1649	October .	1765	October .	1853
November	1648	November.	1751	November.	1859
December .	1688	December .	1773	December .	1944
1927		**1930**		**1933**	
January .	1694	January .	1767	January .	1943
February .	1653	February .	1714	February .	1917
March .	1632	March .	1682	March .	1886
April .	1642	April .	1712	April .	1891
May ..	1650	May .	1742	May .	1904
June .	1685	June .	1788	June .	1939
July .	1682	July .	1794	July .	1934
August .	1669	August .	1767	August .	1927
September	1668	September	1764	September	1919
October .	1710	October .	1791	October .	1912
November	1694	November.	1801	November.	1889
December .	1729	December .	1839	December .	1903

The above statistics are monthly averages, relating to the nine London Clearing Banks, and have been compiled from the *Bulletins* of the *London and Cambridge Economic Service*.

TABLE 21

NEW YORK CITY

AVERAGE RATE OF INTEREST ON CALL LOANS

Year and Month	Call Rate	Year and Month	Call Rate	Year and Month	Call Rate
1925		**1928**		**1931**	
January .	3·32	January .	4·24	January .	1·50
February .	3·60	February .	4·38	February .	1·50
March .	3·97	March .	4·47	March .	1·56
April .	3·86	April .	5·08	April .	1·57
May .	3·82	May .	5·70	May .	1·45
June .	3·97	June .	6·32	June .	1·50
July .	4·09	July .	6·05	July .	1·50
August .	4·19	August .	6·87	August .	1·50
September	4·62	September	7·26	September	1·50
October .	4·87	October .	6·98	October .	2·10
November	4·74	November.	6·67	November.	2·50
December .	5·32	December .	8·86	December .	2·73
1926		**1929**		**1932**	
January .	4·33	January .	6·94	January .	2·65
February .	4·85	February .	7·47	February .	2·50
March .	4·55	March .	9·80	March .	2·50
April .	4·06	April .	9·46	April .	2·50
May .	3·81	May .	8·79	May .	2·50
June .	4·15	June .	7·83	June .	2·50
July .	4·27	July .	9·41	July .	2·08
August .	4·52	August .	8·15	August .	2·00
September	5·02	September	8·62	September	2·00
October .	4·75	October .	6·10	October .	1·35
November	4·56	November.	5·40	November.	1·00
December .	5·16	December .	4·88	December .	1·00
1927		**1930**		**1933**	
January .	4·32	January .	4·31	January .	1·00
February .	4·03	February .	4·28	February .	1·00
March .	4·13	March .	3·56	March .	3·27
April .	4·18	April .	3·79	April . .	1·29
May .	4·26	May .	3·05	May .	1·00
June .	4·33	June .	2·60	June .	1·00
July .	4·05	July .	2·18	July .	1·00
August .	3·68	August .	2·22	August .	0·98
September	3·80	September	2·17	September	0·75
October .	3·90	October .	2·00	October .	0·75
November	3·60	November.	2·00 ·	November.	0·75
December .	4·43	December .	2·27	December .	0·94

These figures represent the monthly average rate of interest paid on new Stock Exchange call loans in New York City and have been compiled from various issues of the *Federal Reserve Bulletin*.

THE GREAT DEPRESSION

TABLE 22

UNITED STATES

INDEX OF COMPOSITE WAGES

(1913 = 100)

Year and Month	Index	Year and Month	Index	Year and Month	Index
1925		**1928**		**1931**	
January .	212	January .	221	January .	212
February .	212	February .	220	February .	213
March .	212	March .	220	March .	213
April .	211	April .	220	April .	212
May .	211	May .	221	May .	209
June .	211	June .	222	June .	207
July .	213	July .	222	July .	207
August .	213	August .	222	August .	206
September	212	September	222	September	202
October .	214	October .	224	October .	199
November	216	November.	224	November.	199
December .	216	December .	224	December .	196
1926		**1929**		**1932**	
January .	217	January .	224	January .	194
February .	216	February .	224	February .	192
March .	216	March .	225	March .	190
April .	218	April .	225	April .	187
May .	217	May .	225	May .	184
June .	218	June .	226	June .	182
July .	219	July .	226	July .	179
August .	218	August .	226	August .	179
September	218	September	227	September	179
October .	220	October .	226	October .	178
November	219	November.	226	November.	177
December .	220	December .	225	December .	174
1927		**1930**		**1933**	
January .	221	January .	226	January .	173
February .	221	February .	225	February ..	172
March .	221	March .	224	March .	168
April .	220	April .	224	April .	170
May .	220	May .	222	May .	172
June .	220	June .	223	June .	173
July .	221	July .	221	July .	176
August .	221	August .	220	August .	177
September	220	September	219	September	177
October .	220	October .	216	October .	177
November	219	November.	216		
December .	221	December .	213		

The above series is a weighted index based on indices of *either* wages *or* earnings in 12 different industries, with seasonal fluctuations eliminated. The index was compiled by the Federal Reserve Bank of New York.

TABLE 23

REICHSBANK

GOLD RESERVES PLUS FOREIGN ASSETS

Millions of Reichsmarks

Year and Month	Reserves	Year and Month	Reserves	Year and Month	Reserves
1925		**1928**		**1931**	
January	1112	January	2161	January	2443
February	1209	February	2170	February	2451
March	1337	March	2120	March	2511
April	1352	April	2209	April	2539
May	1355	May	2315	May	2576
June	1416	June	2334	June	1721
July	1472	July	2384	July	1609
August	1495	August	2443	August	1722
September	1494	September	2576	September	1440
October	1555	October	2696	October	1276
November	1609	November	2796	November	1175
December	1611	December	2884	December	1156
1926		**1929**		**1932**	
January	1673	January	2881	January	1093
February	1843	February	2819	February	1077
March	1972	March	2719	March	1021
April	1883	April	1991	April	990
May	1880	May	2064	May	992
June	1817	June	2272	June	962
July	1988	July	2482	July	894
August	1991	August	2491	August	925
September	2120	September	2547	September	929
October	2129	October	2588	October	940
November	2173	November	2637	November	937
December	2350	December	2687	December	920
1927		**1930**		**1933**	
January	2256	January	2694	January	923
February	2038	February	2828	February	921
March	2055	March	2883	March	836
April	2021	April	2893	April	510
May	1895	May	2942	May	449
June	1870	June	3078	June	274
July	1980	July	2880	July	323
August	2010	August	2988	August	381
September	2006	September	2649	September	407
October	2012	October	2378	October	414
November	2139	November	2705	November	408
December	2147	December	2685	December	395

The above data represent holdings at the end of the month of gold reserves plus those foreign assets which may legally replace gold as primary cover for notes.

TABLE 24

GERMANY

TOTAL CREDITS OF THE BIG BANKS [1]

Millions of Reichsmarks

Year and Month	Credits	Year and Month	Credits	Year and Month	Credits
1925		**1928**		**1931**	
January .	..	January .	..	January .	..
February .	4,205	February .	9,096	February .	10,656
March .	..	March .	9,125	March .	10,688
April .	4,563	April .	9,400	April .	10,569
May .	..	May .	9,545	May .	10,293
June .	4,677	June .	9,532	June .	9,264
July .	.:	July .	9,565	July .	8,156
August .	4,783	August .	9,610	August .	8,002
September	..	September	9,979	September	7,856
October .	5,003	October .	10,309	October .	7,451
November	..	November	10,593	November	7,333
December .	5,227	December .	11,132	December .	..
1926		**1929**		**1932**	
January .	..	January .	..	January .	..
February .	5,241	February .	11,260	February .	7,179
March .	..	March .	11,238	March .	7,198
April .	5,500	April .	10,870	April .	7,171
May .	..	May .	10,513	May .	7,201
June .	5,674	June .	10,818	June .	7,207
July .	..	July .	10,896	July .	7,120
August .	5,935	August .	11,096	August .	7,069
September	..	September	11,395	September	7,110
October .	6,387	October .	11,670	October .	7,067
November	..	November	11,686	November	6,984
December .	6,890	December .	12,001	December .	..
1927		**1930**		**1933**	
January .	..	January .	..	January .	..
February .	7,275	February .	12,004	February .	6,843
March .	..	March .	12,225	March .	6,792
April .	7,569	April .	12,184	April .	6,658
May .	..	May .	12,167	May .	6,537
June .	7,451	June .	12,249	June .	6,502
July .	..	July .	11,989	July .	6,376
August .	7,690	August .	11,739	August .	6,292
September	..	September	11,585	September	6,237
October .	8,121	October .	11,043	October .	6,224
November	..	November	11,021	November	6,216
December .	8,800	December .	11,070	December .	..

[1] *Grossbanken: Kreditoren Insgesamt.*—The above statistics, which relate to the end of the month, include figures for ten banks until February 1929; then, as a result of fusions, nine banks until October 1929; subsequently, seven banks. The series is, however, quite continuous. The data have been compiled from various issues of the *Vierteljahrshefte zur Konjunkturforschung*, published by the German *Institut für Konjunkturforschung*.

TABLE 25

GERMANY—ESTIMATED BALANCE OF PAYMENTS [1]

Millions of Reichsmarks

	1924	1925	1926	1927	1928	1929	1930	Total 1924–30
Exports [2] . . .	7·9	9·5	10·7	11·1	12·6	13·6	12·1	77·5
Imports [2] . . .	9·7	12·0	9·9	14·1	13·9	13·6	10·6	83·8
Balance of Commodity Trade [2] . . .	− 1·8	− 2·5	+ 0·8	− 3·0	− 1·3	..	+ 1·5	− 6·3
Gold and Devisen Movements at Banks of Issue . . .	− 1·3	− 0·1	− 0·5	+ 0·5	− 0·9	+ 0·1	+ 0·1	− 2·1
Reparations . .	− 0·3	− 1·0	− 1·2	− 1·6	− 2·0	− 2·5	− 1·7	− 10·3
Services [3] (Shipping, Tourist, Insurance, etc.) . . .	+ 0·3	+ 0·5	+ 0·5	+ 0·5	+ 0·5	+ 0·5	+ 0·2	+ 3·0
Interest . . .	+ 0·2	..	− 0·2	− 0·3	− 0·6	− 0·8	− 0·8	− 2·5
	− 2·9	− 3·1	− 0·6	− 3·9	− 4·3	− 2·7	− 0·7	− 18·2
Capital Movements— Long term [4] . .	+ 1·0	+ 1·1	+ 1·4	+ 1·7	+ 1·7	+ 0·6	+ 1·6	+ 9·1
Short term [4] . .	+ 1·5	+ 0·3	+ 0·1	+ 1·8	+ 1·4	+ 1·1	..	+ 6·2
Other capital movements, etc. . .	+ 0·4	+ 1·7	− 0·9	+ 0·4	+ 1·2	+ 1·0	− 0·9	+ 2·9
	+ 2·9	+ 3·1	+ 0·6	+ 3·9	+ 4·3	+ 2·7	+ 0·7	+ 18·2

[1] Reproduced from the *Economist*, August 22, 1931, Special Supplement, Annex I.
[2] Includes movement of precious metals (other than those at the Banks of Issue) and the bulk of Deliveries in Kind. The latter amount to 4 milliard Reichsmarks for the seven years.
[3] Includes Reparation deliveries outside Germany, and Deliveries in Kind, so far as these are not included in the figures of Merchandise Trade.
[4] So far as known.

TABLE 26

GERMANY

INDICES OF SECURITY PRICES

Year and Month	Index Base 1924–26	Index Base 1928	Year and Month	Index Base 1924–26	Index Base 1928
1927			March .	111	78
January .	158	111	April .	114	81
February .	169	119	May .	114	80
March .	163	115	June .	109	76
April .	175	123	July .	102	72
May .	168	118	August .	95	67
June .	152	107	September	93	66
July .	158	111	October .	87	61
August .	155	109	November.	83	58
September.	148	104	December .	78	55
October .	143	101	**1931**		
November .	128	90	January .	72	51
December .	136	95	February .	77	54
1928			March .	83	58
January .	138	97	April .	84	59
February .	136	96	May . .	74	52
March .	143	100	June .	67	47
April .	147	103			
May .	148	104	**1932**		
June .	144	101	April .	45	32
July .	143	101	May .	46	33
August .	143	101	June .	46	32
September.	141	99	July .	46	33
October .	140	99	August .	49	34
November .	142	100	September	56	39
December .	140	99	October .	54	38
1929			November.	55	39
January .	139	98	December .	59	41
February .	134	94	**1933**		
March .	133	93	January .	61	43
April .	133	94	February .	61	43
May .	128	90	March .	67	47
June .	131	92	April .	71	50
July .	129	90	May .	72	50
August .	127	89	June .	70	49
September.	125	88	July .	67	47
October .	116	82	August .	65	46
November .	112	78	September	61	43
December .	107	76	October .	60	42
1930			November.	62	44
January .	113	79	December .	65	46
February .	113	79			

The above indices are based on the monthly average prices of 212 ordinary industrial shares, the source of the original data being the *Statistisches Reichsamt*. The series based on the years 1924 to 1926 has been compiled from the *Monthly Bulletin of Statistics* of the League of Nations. That based on 1928 has been calculated from this, for purposes of comparison with the German wage index. The Stock Exchange was closed from July 1931 to April 1932.

TABLE 27

GERMANY

INDEX OF WAGES

$(1928 = 100)$

Year and Month	Index	Year and Month	Index	Year and Month	Index
1925		**1928**		**1931**	
January .	84	January .	96	January .	113
February .	84	February .	97	February .	114
March .	87	March .	97	March .	114
April .	89	April .	98	April .	113
May .	92	May .	101	May .	111
June .	91	June .	101	June .	111
July .	89	July .	100	July .	111
August .	91	August .	100	August .	113
September	94	September	101	September	113
October .	94	October .	102	October .	113
November	96	November .	102	November .	113
December .	97	December .	102	December .	113
1926		**1929**		**1932**	
January .	98	January .	102	January .	107
February .	99	February .	101	February .	109
March .	99	March .	100	March .	109
April .	98	April .	102	April .	109
May .	98	May .	104	May .	106
June .	97	June .	104	June .	106
July .	96	July .	104	July .	105
August .	96	August .	104	August .	106
September	97	September	104	September	106
October .	97	October .	104	October .	106
November	96	November .	105	November .	106
December .	96	December .	105	December .	106
1927		**1930**		**1933**	
January .	96	January .	106	January .	107
February .	96	February .	107	February .	107
March .	96	March .	109	March .	107
April .	97	April .	110	April .	106
May .	99	May .	110	May .	105
June .	99	June .	110	June .	104
July .	97	July .	108	July .	104
August .	99	August .	109	August .	104
September	99	September	110	September	103
October .	97	October .	111	October .	102
November	97	November .	112	November .	102
December .	97	December .	113	December .	102

The above indices are monthly weighted averages for skilled workers in 12 occupations and are based on weekly wages until 1931, and upon hourly wages thereafter. The series has been recalculated from the index published by *Wirtschaft und Statistique*, which is based on 1913.

TABLE 28

GERMANY

DISCOUNT RATE OF THE REICHSBANK

Year and Month	Rate	Year and Month	Rate	Year and Month	Rate
1925		**1928**		**1931**	
January .	10	January .	7	January .	5
February .	9	February .	7	February .	5
March .	9	March .	7	March .	5
April .	9	April .	7	April .	5
May .	9	May .	7	May .	5
June .	9	June .	7	June .	7
July .	9	July .	7	July .	10
August .	9	August .	7	August .	10 [1]
September -	9	September	7	September	8
October .	9	October .	7	October .	8
November	9	November	7	November	8
December .	9	December .	7	December .	7
1926		**1929**		**1932**	
January .	8	January .	$6\frac{1}{2}$	January .	7
February .	8	February .	$6\frac{1}{2}$	February .	7
March .	7	March .	$6\frac{1}{2}$	March .	6
April .	7	April .	$7\frac{1}{2}$	April .	5
May .	7	May .	$7\frac{1}{2}$	May .	5
June .	$6\frac{1}{2}$	June .	$7\frac{1}{2}$	June .	5
July .	6	July .	$7\frac{1}{2}$	July .	5
August .	6	August .	$7\frac{1}{2}$	August .	5
September	6	September	$7\frac{1}{2}$	September	4
October .	6	October .	$7\frac{1}{2}$	October .	4
November	6	November	7	November	4
December .	6	December .	7	December .	4
1927		**1930**		**1933**	
January .	5	January .	$6\frac{1}{2}$	January .	4
February .	5	February .	6	February .	4
March .	5	March .	5	March .	4
April .	5	April .	5	April .	4
May .	5	May .	$4\frac{1}{2}$	May .	4
June .	6	June .	4	June .	4
July .	6	July .	4	July .	4
August .	6	August .	4	August .	4
September	6	September	4	September	4
October .	7	October .	5	October .	4
November	7	November	5	November	4
December .	7	December .	5	December .	4

The above data relate to the end of each month.
[1] The rate rose to 15 per cent during this month.

TABLE 29

NEW YORK FEDERAL RESERVE BANK

DISCOUNT RATE [1]

Year and Month	Rate	Year and Month	Rate	Year and Month	Rate
1925		**1928**		**1931**	
January .	3	January .	3·5	January .	2
February .	3·5	February .	4	February .	2
March .	3·5	March .	4	March .	2
April .	3·5	April .	4	April .	2
May .	3·5	May .	4·5	May .	1·5
June .	3·5	June .	4·5	June .	1·5
July .	3·5	July .	5	July .	1·5
August .	3·5	August .	5	August .	1·5
September	3·5	September	5	September	1·5
October .	3·5	October .	5	October .	3·5 [2]
November	3·5	November	5	November	3·5
December .	3·5	December .	5	December .	3·5
1926		**1929**		**1932**	
January .	4	January .	5	January .	3·5
February .	4	February .	5	February .	3
March .	4	March .	5	March .	3
April .	3·5	April .	5	April .	3
May .	3·5	May .	5	May .	3
June .	3·5	June .	5	June .	2·5
July .	3·5	July .	5	July .	2·5
August .	4	August .	5	August .	2·5
September	4	September	5	September	2·5
October .	4	October .	5	October .	2·5
November	4	November	4·5	November	2·5
December .	4	December .	4·5	December .	2·5
1927		**1930**		**1933**	
January .	4	January .	4·5	January .	2·5
February .	4	February .	4	February .	2·5
March .	4	March .	3·5	March .	3·5
April .	4	April .	3·5	April .	3
May .	4	May .	3	May .	2·5
June .	4	June .	2·5	June .	2·5
July .	4	July .	2·5	July .	2·5
August .	3·5	August .	2·5	August .	2·5
September	3·5	September	2·5	September	2·5
October .	3·5	October .	2·5	October .	2
November	3·5	November	2·5	November	2
December .	3·5	December .	2	December .	2

[1] Discount Rate for 60- to 90-day commercial paper. For the first three years the rates given are monthly averages. Thereafter, they relate to the end of the month.

[2] From 8th to 14th October, 2·5 per cent.

TABLE 30

BANK OF ENGLAND—BANK RATE

Year and Month	Rate	Year and Month	Rate	Year and Month	Rate
1925		**1928**		**1931**	
January .	4	January .	4·5	January .	3
February .	4	February .	4·5	February .	3
March .	5	March .	4·5	March .	3
April .	5	April .	4·5	April .	3
May .	5	May .	4·5	May .	2·5
June .	5	June .	4·5	June .	2·5
July .	5	July .	4·5	July .	4·5 [2]
August .	4·5	August .	4·5	August .	4·5
September	4·5	September	4·5	September	6
October .	4	October .	4·5	October .	6
November	4	November .	4·5	November .	6
December .	5	December .	4·5	December .	6
1926		**1929**		**1932**	
January .	5	January .	4·5	January .	6
February .	5	February .	5·5	February .	5
March .	5	March .	5·5	March .	3·5 [3]
April .	5	April .	5·5	April .	3
May .	5	May .	5·5	May .	2·5
June .	5	June .	5·5	June .	2
July .	5	July .	5·5	July .	2
August .	5	August .	5·5	August .	2
September	5	September	6·5	September	2
October .	5	October .	6	October .	2
November	5	November .	5·5	November .	2
December .	5	December .	5	December .	2
1927		**1930**		**1933**	
January .	5	January .	5	January .	2
February .	5	February .	4·5	February .	2
March .	5	March .	3·5 [1]	March .	2
April .	4·5	April .	3·5	April .	2
May .	4·5	May .	3	May .	2
June .	4·5	June .	3	June .	2
July .	4·5	July .	3	July .	2
August .	4·5	August .	3	August .	2
September	4·5	September	3	September	2
October .	4·5	October .	3	October .	2
November	4·5	November .	3	November .	2
December .	4·5	December .	3	December .	2

Monthly averages for the first three years, then end-of-the-month data—
[1] From 6th to 19th March, 4 per cent.
[2] From 23rd to 29th July, 3·5 per cent.
[3] From 9th to 15th March, 4 per cent.

TABLE 31

BANK OF FRANCE—DISCOUNT RATE

Year and Month	Rate	Year and Month	Rate	Year and Month	Rate
1925		**1928**		**1931**	
January	7	January	3·5	January	2
February	7	February	3·5	February	2
March	7	March	3·5	March	2
April	7	April	3·5	April	2
May	7	May	3·5	May	2
June	7	June	3·5	June	2
July	6	July	3·5	July	2
August	6	August	3·5	August	2
September	6	September	3·5	September	2
October	6	October	3·5	October	2·5
November	6	November	3·5	November	2·5
December	6	December	3·5	December	2·5
1926		**1929**		**1932**	
January	6	January	3·5	January	2·5
February	6	February	3·5	February	2·5
March	6	March	3·5	March	2·5
April	6	April	3·5	April	2·5
May	6	May	3·5	May	2·5
June	6	June	3·5	June	2·5
July	7·5	July	3·5	July	2·5
August	7·5	August	3·5	August	2·5
September	7·5	September	3·5	September	2·5
October	7·5	October	3·5	October	2·5
November	7·5	November	3·5	November	2·5
December	6·5	December	3·5	December	2·5
1927		**1930**		**1933**	
January	6·5	January	3	January	2·5
February	5·5	February	3	February	2·5
March	5·5	March	3	March	2·5
April	5	April	2·5	April	2·5
May	5	May	2·5	May	2·5
June	5	June	2·5	June	2·5
July	5	July	2·5	July	2·5
August	5	August	2·5	August	2·5
September	5	September	2·5	September	2·5
October	5	October	2·5	October	2·5
November	5	November	2·5	November	2·5
December	4	December	2·5	December	2·5

For the first three years, the rates given are monthly averages. Thereafter, they relate to the end of the month.

TABLE 32

STERLING-DOLLAR EXCHANGE

LONDON QUOTATIONS

Year and Month	Rate	Year and Month	Rate	Year and Month	Rate
1925		**1928**		**1931**	
January	4·780	January	4·876	January	4·855
February	4·772	February	4·875	February	4·857
March	4·777	March	4·880	March	4·859
April	4·796	April	4·882	April	4·860
May	4·855	May	4·882	May	4·864
June	4·861	June	4·881	June	4·865
July	4·860	July	4·864	July	4·857
August	4·857	August	4·854	August	4·857
September	4·847	September	4·851	September	4·542
October	4·843	October	4·850	October	3·886
November	4·846	November	4·850	November	3·719
December	4·850	December	4·853	December	3·372
1926		**1929**		**1932**	
January	4·858	January	4·850	January	3·430
February	4·864	February	4·853	February	3·459
March	4·861	March	4·853	March	3·634
April	4·862	April	4·853	April	3·752
May	4·862	May	4·851	May	3·676
June	4·866	June	4·849	June	3·649
July	4·864	July	4·851	July	3·552
August	4·858	August	4·849	August	3·476
September	4·855	September	4·848	September	3·471
October	4·850	October	4·870	October	3·399
November	4·849	November	4·878	November	3·277
December	4·851	December	4·882	December	3·276
1927		**1930**		**1933**	
January	4·853	January	4·870	January	3·372
February	4·850	February	4·862	February	3·422
March	4·854	March	4·863	March	3·436
April	4·857	April	4·863	April	3·507
May	4·857	May	4·860	May	3·938
June	4·856	June	4·859	June	4·141
July	4·855	July	4·865	July	4·643
August	4·861	August	4·871	August	4·503
September	4·863	September	4·861	September	4·660
October	4·870	October	4·859	October	4·667
November	4·874	November	4·857	November	5·136
December	4·883	December	4·857	December	5·124

The above are monthly averages of daily rates, and have been compiled from the *Bulletins* of the *London and Cambridge Economic Service*.

TABLE 33

STERLING-DOLLAR EXCHANGE 1914 TO 1933—NEW YORK QUOTATIONS

Month	1914	1915	1916	1917	1918	1919	1920	1921	1922	1923	1924	1925	1926	1927	1928	1929	1930	1931	1932	1933
Jan.	..	4·8537	4·7800	4·7585	4·7535	4·7658	3·6779	3·7419	4·2247	4·6546	4·2591	4·7816	4·8578	4·8526	4·8753	4·8498	4·8688	4·8546	3·4312	3·3613
Feb.	..	4·8495	4·7662	4·7580	4·7535	4·7648	3·3810	3·8758	4·3620	4·6908	4·3077	4·7724	4·8633	4·8502	4·8748	4·8521	4·8617	4·8583	3·4563	3·4220
Mar.	..	4·8125	4·7650	4·7555	4·7535	4·7147	3·7258	3·9111	4·3757	4·6956	4·2906	4·7762	4·8608	4·8540	4·8799	4·8526	4·8631	4·8583	3·6303	3·4328
April	..	4·8000	4·7650	4·7585	4·7550	4·6617	3·9310	3·9292	4·4133	4·6554	4·3512	4·7953	4·8622	4·8565	4·8820	4·8532	4·8631	4·8598	3·7499	3·5793
May	..	4·8000	4·7625	4·7556	4·7550	4·6678	3·8477	3·9753	4·4461	4·6256	4·3608	4·8547	4·8615	4·8570	4·8816	4·8507	4·8596	4·8040	3·6751	3·0323
June	4·8910	4·7856	4·7587	4·7555	4·7550	4·6211	3·9497	3·7815	4·4518	4·6146	4·3198	4·8604	4·8661	4·8561	4·8802	4·8482	4·8586	4·8648	3·6466	4·1356
July	5·5000	4·7712	4·7587	4·7565	4·7535	4·4287	3·8647	3·6321	4·4463	4·5833	4·3703	4·8596	4·8634	4·8550	4·8636	4·8510	4·8656	4·8560	3·5495	4·6499
Aug.	5·5600	4·7625	4·7587	4·7555	4·7600	4·2720	3·6219	3·6536	4·4646	4·5603	4·4994	4·8569	4·8586	4·8602	4·8535	4·8485	4·8707	4·8577	3·4757	4·5026
Sept.	5·0625	4·7300	4·7075	4·7555	4·7550	4·1790	3·5102	3·7240	4·4307	4·5422	4·4605	4·8464	4·8541	4·8635	4·8505	4·8482	4·8611	4·5312	3·4710	4·6647
Oct.	4·9800	4·7250	4·7569	4·7530	4·7550	4·1840	3·4751	3·8728	4·4384	4·5237	4·4870	4·8428	4·8503	4·8696	4·8495	4·8699	4·8589	3·8893	3·3961	4·6683
Nov.	4·9087	4·7137	4·7175	4·7520	4·7375	4·0982	3·4872	3·9702	4·4799	4·3821	4·6096	4·8458	4·8487	4·8740	4·8492	4·8774	4·8564	3·7199	3·2752	5·1497
Dec.	4·8925	4·7512	4·7569	4·7525	4·7585	3·8123	3·4923	4·1561	4·6098	4·3601	4·6958	4·8498	4·8512	4·8825	4·8524	4·8816	4·8566	3·3737	3·2786	5·1158
An. Av.	..	..	..	..	..	4·4258	3·6642	3·8490	4·4292	4·5748	4·4171	4·8289	4·8582	4·8610	4·8662	4·8568	4·8621	4·5349	3·5060	4·2368

The above statistics have been compiled from various issues of the *Federal Reserve Bulletin*. For the period prior to 1919 they represent the highest rate for sight drafts during the month; for 1919 and subsequent years the figures given are monthly averages of buying rates for cable transfers.

TABLE 34

UNITED KINGDOM—INDEX OF AVERAGE WEEKLY WAGES

(Dec. 1924 = 100)

Month	1919	1920	1921	1922	1923	1924	1925	1926	1927	1928	1929	1930	1931	1932	1933
January	115	128	155	121	99	96.5	100.5	100.5	101	100.5	99.5	99	98	96	94.5
February	116	128	154	120	99	97	100.5	100.5	101	100	99.5	98.5	97.5	95.5	94
March	116	131	154	120	99	98	101	100.5	101	100	99.5	98.5	97.5	95.5	94
April	116	131	(151)	115	99	98	101	100.5	101	100	99.5	98.5	97	95.5	94
May	117	141	(150)	113	99	99	101	100.5	100.5	100	99.5	98.25	97	95.5	94
June	117	146	(147)	110	98	100	100	100.5	100.5	100	99.5	98.25	97	95.5	94
July	121	147	141	108	97	100	100.5	100	100	100	99.5	98	97	95.25	94
August	121	149	136	107	97	100	100.5	100	101	99.5	99.5	98	96.75	95.25	94
September	122	151	132	101	97	100	100.5	100	101	99.5	99	98	96.75	95.25	94
October	122	151	130	101	97	100	100.5	100	100.5	99.5	99	98	96.5	95	94
November	123	153	127	100	97	100	100.5	100.5	100.5	99.5	99	98	96.5	94.5	94
December	126	154	125	99	96.5	100	100.5	101	100.5	99.5	99	98	96.5	94.5	94
An. Av.	119	142.5	142	109	98	99	100.5	100.5	100.75	100	99.5	98.25	97	95.25	94

From 1924 onwards, the above series is Professor Bowley's Index of Average Weekly Wages, based on December 1924, as published by the *London and Cambridge Economic Service*. For the period prior to 1924 Professor Bowley's earlier series, based on 1913, has been recalculated on the 1924 base. The two sections are, therefore, not strictly comparable. For a full description of the new series see *Special Memorandum No. 28*, of the *London and Cambridge Economic Service*.

TABLE 35

UNITED KINGDOM

BALANCE OF PAYMENTS ON INCOME ACCOUNT

Item	1925	1926	1927	1928	1929	1930	1931
Credits (£ millions)							
Exports of British Produce . .	773	653	709	724	729	571	389
Exports of Silver Coin and Bullion .	12	11	7	9	9	8	7
Exports of Gold Coin and Bullion .	50	27	29	61	78	82	133
Estimated net National Shipping Income	124	120	140	130	130	105	80
Estimated net Income from Overseas Investment	250	250	250	250	250	220	165
Estimated net Income from Short Interest and Commissions	60	60	63	65	65	55	30
Estimated net Receipts from Other Sources . . .	15	15	15	15	15	15	10
Net Excess of Government Receipts .	..	4	1	15	24	19	16
TOTAL . .	1284	1140	1214	1269	1300	1075	830
Debits (£ millions)							
Retained Imports of Merchandise .	1167	1116	1095	1075	1111	957	798
Imports of Silver Coin and Bullion .	11	11	7	10	8	9	8
Imports of Gold Coin and Bullion .	41	39	32	48	62	87	98
Net Excess of Government Payments .	11	..	..	..	..	..	..
TOTAL . .	1230	1166	1134	1133	1181	1053	904
Credit (+) or Debit (−) on above items [1]	+ 54	− 26	+ 79	+ 137	+ 118	+ 23	− 75

The above Table is reproduced from Benham, *British Monetary Policy*, London, 1932, p. 14.

[1] Most of these differ by £1 million from the difference between total credits and total debits as shown. This is because decimal points have been omitted. The net credits and debits as shown are correct.

TABLE 36

FOREIGN EXCHANGE RATES

PERCENTAGE DISCOUNT IN RELATION TO GOLD PARITY

Year	Argentina	Australia	Canada	Japan	Spain	Sweden	U.K.
1931							
January .	27·75	..	·21	·81	..	·13	·24
February	25·43	..	·02	·88	..	·11	·17
March .	19·11	..	·02	·96	..	·08	·17
April .	20·74	..	·05	·98	..	·09	·14
May .	26·71	..	·06	·93	..	·03 [1]	·05
June .	27·18	..	·28	·95	..	·02 [1]	·03
July .	27·56	..	·34	·99	..	·16	·22
August .	33·07	23·37	·31	·99	54·41	·19	·18
September	38·12	28·51	3·75	1·03	53·44	2·66	6·89
October .	46·10	38·64	10·90	1·19	53·55	13·75	20·08
November	39·01	41·31	11·01	1·10	55·36	22·62	23·56
December	39·34	44·83	17·29	2·80	56·47	30·18	30·68
1932							
January .	39·60	43·71	14·87	27·80	56·50	28·40	29·49
February	39·65	43·30	12·71	31·14	59·75	28·01	28·98
March .	39·58	40·29	10·55	35·49	60·62	25·92	25·22
April .	39·66	38·48	10·12	34·18	60·12	28·76	22·94
May .	39·55	39·71	11·56	35·86	57·93	30·13	24·48
June .	39·34	40·17	13·26	39·24	57·27	30·20	25·07
July .	39·30	41·77	12·93	44·94	58·27	32·02	27·06
August .	39·29	42·98	12·45	50·86	58·22	33·40	28·58
September	39·27	43·05	9·74	52·59	58·00	33·56	28·68
October .	39·28	44·28	8·77	53·73	57·57	34·57	30·21
November	39·28	46·27	12·70	58·63	57·64	34·96	32·70
December	39·28	46·21	13·40	58·41	57·76	33·17	32·63
1933							
January .	39·28	44·85	12·54	58·39	57·62	31·72	30·67
February	39·28	43·86	16·49	58·28	57·27	31·84	29·72
March .	39·57	43·96	16·48	57·34	56·24	32·13	29·58
April .	39·65	44·10	19·08	57·68	56·04	32·96	29·73
May .	39·96	45·12	25·27	58·93	55·84	35·57	31·16
June .	39·93	44·83	26·69	57·85	56·19	35·23	30·68
July .	39·95	45·52	32·20	58·57	56·65	35·78	31·41
August .	39·98	46·36	31·28	60·66	56·72	36·83	32·48
September	39·86	48·58	34·97	63·15	56·65	39·50	35·31
October .	39·87	48·59	34·26	62·48	56·59	39·51	35·47
November	40·36	47·37	36·75	61·39	57·52	38·07	33·86
December	49·71	46·41	35·65	60·53	57·57	36·97	32·70

The above Table has been compiled from various issues of the League of Nations' *Monthly Bulletin of Statistics.*

[1] Premium.

CPSIA information can be obtained at www.ICGtesting.com
Printed in the USA
LVOW10s2228010315

428867LV00002B/203/P

9 781412 810081